Contents

A Forgiving Heart

Prayers for Blessing and Reconciliation

Edited by
Lyn Klug

Augsburg Books
MINNEAPOLIS

A FORGIVING HEART
Prayers for Blessing and Reconciliation

Large-quantity purchases or custom editions of this book are available at a discount from the publisher. For more information, contact the sales department at Augsburg Fortress, Publishers, 1-800-328-4648, or write to: Sales Director, Augsburg Fortress, Publishers, P.O. Box 1209, Minneapolis, MN 55440-1209.

Scripture passages are from the New Revised Standard Version of the Bible, copyright © 1946, 1952, 1971, 1989 by the Division of Christian Education of the National Council of the Churches of Christ in the USA. Used by permission. Acknowledgment of copyrighted material begins on page 186.

Library of Congress Cataloging-in-Publication Data
A forgiving heart : prayers for blessing and reconciliation / [edited]
by Lyn Klug.
   p. cm.
 ISBN 0-8066-3997-0 (pbk. : alk. paper)
 1. Forgiveness—Prayer-books and devotions—English. I. Klug, Lyn.
BV283.F67 2003
242'.8—dc21   2002152839

Cover and book design by Michelle L. N. Cook
Cover art from Eyewire

The paper used in this publication meets the minimum requirements of American National Standard for Information Sciences—Permanence of Paper for Printed Library Materials, ANSI Z329.48-1984. ♾ ™

Manufactured in Canada

07   06   05   04   03   1   2   3   4   5   6   7   8   9   10

Introduction

All of us give and receive love. All of us fail to give and receive love. Forgiveness makes love possible because it is an intentional change of attitude about those failures. Forgiveness leaves the future open, creates the opportunity to grow in love, and heals what years of running away, defending, and blaming cannot heal.

Forgiveness is a way of life that Jesus spent much of his ministry teaching. One Gospel story after another is about sin, repentance, confession, reconciliation, and blessing. The prayers and readings in this book are based on those teachings.

Even people who know the biblical teachings well have many questions about how to live them out. How can I know that I've forgiven or been forgiven? Why should I try to forgive? Will anything be different? Can we forgive ourselves? Can I forgive someone who neither admits nor regrets what they did? What if I've been harmed by a group or institution—is forgiveness possible then? How important is confession and to whom should I confess? Can prayer really make a difference? Are some things unforgivable? Does forgiving mean I must try to forget? Is reconciliation always possible or even desirable?

Answers to these questions do not appear in this book. But if you use the readings for reflection and prayer, the answers will appear in your life. No situation that is prayed for stays the same.

Contemporary writers on forgiveness often describe a series of stages, much like the stages of grief or dying. These stages are not predictable, nor do they happen in order. The process is complex, and only our experience will teach us. Each situation and each person is unique.

How would it feel to live without the hazardous waste of our conflicts and hurts? Can we even imagine such a gift? People who have forgiven describe their sense of freedom, peace, inner strength, and the joy of living in the present instead of the past. Their feelings and actions aren't hostage to someone else. They are less tense, less defensive, more relaxed. They also know that they will be hurt again, that being hurt is a part of life. But they're better prepared.

Christians have long been aware that forgiveness is crucial to social change. Advances in peacemaking, civil rights, community building, and restorative justice depend on it. Pastors, therapists, and friends help people to forgive in their everyday relationships. Research in the medical and social sciences is beginning to confirm the importance of forgiveness in mental and physical health, end-of-life issues, living with disabilities, healing from abuse of all kinds, crime prevention, addiction, and international politics, even when war and genocide have taken place. Forgiveness is important because it's powerful, not because it's passive. It takes courage, strength, and faith.

Some ways to pray about forgiveness

The most important kind of prayer is what you normally do. You may pray using Bible passages or devotional books, journal, meditate, talk spontaneously to God. You may pray with few words. A writer friend said recently, "Most of my praying about this situation has been wordless agony."

Lectio divina, or divine reading, is a way of praying that helps us be more attentive to what God might be saying to us, especially if we are in need of comfort and guidance.

1. Read an entire prayer slowly, out loud if possible.
2. Take some deep breaths and sit quietly for a few minutes.
3. Read the prayer again. Why did you choose it? What part are you responding to? Be comfortable with silence between thoughts.
4. Read the prayer once more. Be quiet. Be open to its effect on you. Where is God leading?
5. Trust that whatever you experience during this time, God's grace is at work in you.

Another way to meditate on a prayer involves even fewer words and less thinking:

1. Read the prayer slowly.
2. Choose a word or short phrase that attracts your attention.
3. Why is this phrase meaningful? How does it relate to your life?
4. Silently repeat the phrase in rhythm with your breathing. For example, *Breathing in:* "I bless and release you"/ *Breathing out:* "to the Holy Spirit."
5. As you breathe the prayer, you may become aware of an image, a feeling, a sense of God's presence, a desire to do something. At the very least, you are replacing thoughts of worry, fear, or hostility with words of trust and faith in the promises of God.
6. Be silent, resting in God's presence, focusing only on your breath as it flows in and out.
7. Close with the Lord's Prayer or any other prayer you know by heart. Some of the blessing prayers in this book would work well.

Loving kindness prayer connects us with the feelings of compassion that we already have for those we love, and then extends these same feelings to people we find it more difficult to pray for— enemies, possibly, or strangers who are in trouble. These prayers are found on pages 46–47, 55, and 56.

Guided meditation, rituals, journaling, and Bible study are all helpful in becoming a more forgiving person. Stories of people in similar situations to your own are often the most transforming experiences of all. The suggested readings in the acknowledgments are some of the best books that I found. There are also excellent recent books about forgiveness in the healing of abuse, violent crime, battering, and other especially difficult life experiences.

Making the prayers your own

If you keep a journal, record any responses, feelings, insights, or actions you would like to take. You may want to write your own prayers, or expand some of them by thinking further along the lines suggested.

In the past, the image of God as Father conveyed positive attributes of caring, unconditional love, and reliability. Today we use many other images for God as well. Some prayers have the personal pronoun "me," some "us," and some "you." These are interchangeable.

The prayers we can't pray are often very significant. What does it mean that I am sitting here with words I can't say, don't believe, or don't want to believe? Why do I want to turn the page and forget about them? Can I sit with the prayer awhile, not analyzing, but just allowing the thoughts in?

The effects of prayer will never be lost through honesty. There will be no end to seeking understanding or asking questions or doubting ourselves and God. But there will also be hope, trust, and the peace of a forgiving heart.

Ways to use prayer books

Most of these prayers are meant for personal reflection rather than public use. But with some simple changes, many could be used in a variety of settings.

- praying with another person
- praying in a group
- mailings and meetings of your church's prayer chain
- church committee meetings
- adult education groups
- traditional and contemporary worship
- special worship services, especially those with a peace and justice, national, or global emphasis
- mission events
- men and women's gatherings, youth groups
- worship for retreats, or an entire retreat on forgiveness
- ecumenical community services

Send a prayer in a card or E-mail to someone for whom it seems particularly appropriate. Letting a friend know he or she is not alone is often the best gift we can give.

Why use written prayers?

The prayers of others sometimes comfort us, sometimes help us recognize our own unforgiveness and ill will. The anger and grief of another person help me admit mine, and their hope for the future gives me hope.

Frederick Buechner expresses better than anyone the reason why so many of us seek out the words of others, even though we say our own also:

> Words written fifty years ago, a hundred years ago, a thousand years ago, can have as much of this power today as ever they had it then to come alive for us and in us and to make us more alive within ourselves. That, I suppose, is the final mystery as well as the final power of words: that not even across great distances of time and space do they ever lose their capacity for becoming incarnate. And when these words tell of virtue and nobility, when they move us closer to that truth and gentleness of spirit by which we become fully human, the reading of them is sacramental; and a library is as holy a place as any temple is holy, because through the words which are treasured in it the Word itself becomes flesh again and again and dwells among us, full of grace and truth.

Note: If no country is given after a prayer, the writer is from the United States. If no dates are given, he or she is a contemporary. For a list of first lines and sources, please see the acknowledgments beginning on page 186.

Chapter 1

Abiding in God's Love

Beloved, let us love one another, because love is from God; everyone who loves is born of God and knows God.

—1 John 4:7

Return to the Lord, your God, for he is gracious and merciful, slow to anger, and abounding in steadfast love.

—Joel 2:13

Lord, let me return to you,
let me come to you,
reach out to me.
I am alone.
Alone.
Empty-hearted.
Afraid of myself.
Let me come to you.
Reach out to me.

—Chaim Stern, preparatory service for the Days of Awe

Spirit of comfort and longing,
enfold my fear,
unclothe me of my pride,
unweave my thoughts,
uncomplicate my heart,
and give me surrender:
that I may tell my wounds,
lay down my work,
and greet the dark.

—Janet Morley, England

God help us to find our confession;
the truth within us which is hidden from our mind,
the beauty or the ugliness we see elsewhere
but never in ourselves;
the stowaway which has been smuggled
into the dark side of the heart,
which puts the heart off balance and causes it pain,
which wearies and confuses us,
which tips us in false directions and inclines us to destruction,
the load which is not carried squarely
because it is carried in ignorance.
God help us to find our confession.

—Michael Leunig, Australia

O God of grace, give us your grace that we may not savor the evil in others in order to disguise the evil in ourselves. Amen

—The Reverend Jean Dalby Clift

I have knowingly and willingly disobeyed you, Lord, counting on your forgiveness all the while.

Yet, I know that I cannot dodge your judgment.
I know that some choices have to be made.
I have to decide what I want most.

Lord, I want to want to be healed.

—Robert A. Raines

Repentance has nothing to do with self-torment. We must be truly sorry for our sins, but we must also turn from them and look to God. If we look only at ourselves we are sure to despair. Once we have cried our tears of remorse, we must stand back and allow the muddy waters of our hearts to clear—otherwise we will never see to the bottom of anything.

—Johann Christoph Arnold

We must not despair, for there is no sin that exceeds God's compassion. It is always the devil that brings despair. One must not listen.

—Letter from a Russian monk

We come before you today, Lord,
to tell you about all the hazardous waste we are carrying around:
Fear.
Self-pity.
Anger.
Guilt.
Regret.
Perfectionism.
Hatred.
Resentment.
Bitterness.
There isn't one of us who doesn't know the meaning of these
words in a very personal way.
We'd just as soon get rid of all this stuff, but we can't seem
to let go.
If we did, we'd have to change . . . and, Jesus, you know how
we feel about change.
Give us a new concept of change.
Let us see the beauty,
the excitement,
the glory and wonder of change.
Life is change.
If nothing changes, there is death.
We don't want that.
We are here because we choose life.
Help us to act like it. Amen

—Holly Jo Turnquist Fischer

*M*erciful Healer, enter those deep, dark places from which my hurtfulness has come. Touch my hidden wounds, awaken me, set me free, empower me with your new life, enfold me in your mercy. I pray you also heal and enfold those whom I have hurt. I pray in the strong power of your name.

—Flora Slosson Wuellner

*G*od in Heaven, you have helped my life to grow like a tree. Now, something has happened. Satan, like a bird, has carried in one twig of his own choosing after another. Before I knew it he had built a dwelling place and was living in it. Tonight, my Father, I am throwing out both the bird and the nest.

—prayer of a Nigerian Christian

Gracious God, humble us through the violence of your love so we are able to know and confess our sins. We want our sins to be interesting, but, God forgive us, they are so ordinary: envy, hatred, meanness, pride, self-centeredness, laziness, boredom, lying, lust, stinginess and so on. You have saved us from "and so on" to be a royal people able to witness to the world that the powers that make us such ordinary sinners have been defeated. So capture our attention with the beauty of your life that the ugliness of sin may be seen as just that—ugly. God, how wonderful it is to be captivated by you.

—Stanley Hauerwas

For our age prayer must be the bringing of the full self to God: all the sexual and aggressive fantasies, the fears and mediocrity, the petty faults and the major turnings away, the grandiose wishes and secret longings, the laziness, the angers, the buried hopes and desires to give and serve, the caring for other people, the hatred of enemies, the pain of the suffering and unfairness in our world, the bounding into praise and the falling-away into sleep in mid-prayer. All this human stuff—ordered, unordered, disordered—is what we must bring in a big sack and dump out and sort through and talk over with God.

—Ann and Barry Ulanov

We come to you in penitence, confessing our sins: the vows we have forgotten, the opportunities we have let slip, the excuses whereby we have sought to deceive ourselves and you. Forgive us that we talk so much and are silent so seldom, that we are in such constant motion and are so rarely still, that we depend so implicitly on the effectiveness of our organizations and so little on the power of your Spirit. Teach us to wait upon you, that we may renew our strength, mount up with wings as eagles, run and not be weary, walk and not faint.

—William Sloane Coffin, Jr.

Lord Christ, help us to have the courage and humility to name
our burdens
and lay them down
so that we are light to walk across the water
to where you beckon us.

Our pride,
armouring us,
hardening us,
making us defend our dignity by belittling others,
We name it
and we lay it down.

The memory of hurts and insults,
driving us to lash out,
to strike back,
We name it
and we lay it down.

Our antagonism against those
whose actions, differences, presence,
threaten our comfort or security,
We name it
and we lay it down.

Our fear,
of unsolved questions,
of the unknown,
of fear itself,
We name it
and we lay it down.

We do not need these burdens,
but we have grown used to carrying them,
have forgotten what it is like to be light.

Beckon us to lightness of being,
for you show us it is not unbearable.
Only so can we close up the distance
Only so can we walk upon the water.

It is so.

Blessed are you, Lord Christ, who makes heavy burdens light.

Kathy Galloway, Iona, Scotland

I have already confessed my sins to you, God.
I have told you of my wrongdoings
and how bad I feel about them.
You have heard me,
and you have forgiven me.
And yet.
I still carry the memory and the pain of them inside me.
I feel the hot
flush on my cheeks
every time I revisit my words and my actions.
I feel forgiven by you,
but inside I am still bearing the unbearable.
Because I have not told anyone my secret shame,
the secret now feels too shameful to tell.

Help me to find the face that I need.
Help me to pick someone I can tell this to,
who will be kind and patient with me.
Help me to say to someone I can trust,
"I was so awful. I was so selfish. I was so mean,"
and hear that everybody is that way sometimes.
I need even more to see in someone's face
and hear in someone's voice,
that in spite of everything, I am still a good person.
I know I am forgiven,
but I need to see it with my eyes and hear it with my ears.
Send someone to me soon.
Help me recognize the one you send.

—Karen Batdorf

*N*obody has to sit about being humiliated in the outer office while God dispatches important business, before condescending to issue a stamped official discharge accompanied by an improving lecture. Like the Father of the Prodigal Son, God can see repentance coming a great way off and is there to meet it, and the repentance is the reconciliation.

—Dorothy L. Sayers (1893-1957), England

*C*onfess your sins to one another, and pray for one another, so that you may be healed. The prayer of the righteous is powerful and effective.

—James 5:16

I'm weary of being sorry over and over
for the same mistakes.
I've changed as much as I can for now.
Who I am is who I am.
I make promises to myself and to you.
I have wise insights
and generous plans.
But you know and I know
how few of them will make it
out of my journal and into my life.
When I don't live by the light that I have,
how can I ask for more?
But I keep coming back anyway.
I have to trust that my honesty
is an acceptable offering.

    —Lyn Klug

A woman doesn't meet her God every day,
a man doesn't always feel his prayers,
not every hour is one of grace.

We fall, we fail,
to the end of our road.
We turn back only to lose our way yet again,
to wander in search of forgotten paths.

But God, holding a candle,
looks for all who wander, all who search.

　　　—Shifra Alon, translated by Chaim Stern

*T*he voice of despair says, "I sin over and over again. After endless
promises to myself and others to do better next time, I find myself
back again in the old dark places. Forget about trying to change. I
have tried for years. It didn't work and it will never work. It is better
that I get out of people's way, be forgotten, no longer around, dead."

　　　This strangely attractive voice . . . speaks unambiguously for
the darkness and offers a clear-cut negative identity.

But Jesus came to open my ears to another voice that says, "I am
your God, I have molded you with my own hands, and I love what I
have made. I love you with a love that has no limits, because I love
you as I am loved. Do not run away from me. Come back to me—
not once, not twice, but always again. You are my child. How can

you ever doubt that I will embrace you again, hold you against my breast, kiss you and let my hands run through your hair? I am your God—the God of mercy and compassion, the God of pardon and love, the God of tenderness and care. Please do not say that I have given up on you, that I cannot stand you anymore, that there is no way back. It is not true. I so much want you to be with me. I so much want you to be close to me. I know all your thoughts. I hear all your words. I see all of your actions. And I love you because you are beautiful, made in my own image, an expression of my most intimate love. Do not judge yourself. Do not condemn yourself. Do not reject yourself. Let my love touch the deepest, most hidden corners of your heart and reveal to you your own beauty, a beauty that you have lost sight of, but which will become visible to you again in the light of my mercy. Come, come, let me wipe your tears, and let my mouth come close to your ear and say to you, 'I love you, I love you, I love you.'"

—Henri J.M. Nouwen (1932-1996)

No matter how far we have wandered, no matter how much damage we have inflicted on ourselves, God still loves us and still wants what is good for us. That's why God continues to pester us with discontent and uncertainty when we do wrong. That's why God never lets us be fulfilled by anything other than God. That's why God continues to offer us forgiveness.

—Daniel E. Pilarczyk

Peace and love are always in us, being and working,
but we are not always in peace and love.
God is ground of our whole life in Love, and wants us to know this.
God is also our everlasting keeper and wants us to know this.
God is our friend who keeps us tenderly while we are in sin,
and touches us privately, showing us where we went wrong
by the sweet light of compassion and grace,
even though we imagine that we will be punished.

I saw no vengeance in God, not for a short time, nor for a long—
for as I see it, if God were vengeful, even for a brief moment,
we would never have life, place, or being.

In God is endless friendship, space, life, and being.

I knew by the common teaching of Holy Church
and by my own feeling
that the blame for our sins clings to us continually
while we are on this earth.

How amazing it was, then,
to see our God showing us no more blame
than if we were as clean and whole as the Angels in heaven!

    —Julian of Norwich (1342-1419), England

If God pleases to forget anything, then He can forget it. And I think that is what He does with our sins—that is, after He has got them away from us, once we are clean from them altogether. It would be a dreadful thing if He forgot them before that.

—George Macdonald (1824-1905), Scotland

✍❤

When the thought of God does not remind us of our sin but that it is forgiven, and the past is no longer the memory of how much we did wrong, but of how much we were forgiven— then we rest in the forgiveness of sins.

—Søren Kierkegaard (1813-1855), Denmark, alt.

Breathing deeply and slowly, silently say half of a line as you inhale, and half as you exhale. As the prayer is repeated, painful areas of the body may relax and God's loving presence may be experienced deep in the heart.

Breathing in: Just as I am / *breathing out:* I come.

Things overwhelm me. / Come to my help.

Lord Jesus Christ / have mercy on me.

Forgive me those things / of which my conscience is afraid.

Do not look at appearances / but at my heart.

Be patient / with me.

Held in your mercy / held in your love.

Into your hands, O God / into your light.

Though I want to flee from you, / I flee toward you.

Thank you / for the joy of forgiveness.

I have / been given mercy.

*F*orgiveness is not just the cancelling of a debt . . . , still less a "letting off" of all consequence—but the restoration of a relationship so rich and new that I, even I, can lift up my head and look into Your face and, in spite of all the past, say humbly, even to You, in this moment: "There is nothing between us."

　--Leslie Weatherhead (1883-1975), England

*"W*ho is closer to God," the seeker asked, "the saint or the sinner?" "Why the sinner, of course," the elder said. "But how can that be?" the seeker asked. "Because," the elder said, "every time a person sins they break the cord that binds them to God. But every time God forgives them, the cord is knotted again. And so, thanks to the mercy of God, the cord gets shorter and the sinner closer to God."

　—Joan D. Chittister, OSB

Savior, for this long road that has wound, like Your own, through the marshlands of defeat and the lookouts of hope, for this road I pray a blessing. I pray a benediction.

Not only for the high hills but for the valleys of Your redeemed one, the desertions, the weakness, the betrayals—for these too I pray a blessing and a benediction.

That even in my weakness You may be glorified, even in my failure You may succeed, even in my silence You may be praised— for this I pray, Savior also of lost moments.

—Walter Riess

Light breaks upon the heart, and
on sea,
sky, stone.
Its falling is great, beautiful, and new.
And now
in silent song
the angels glow,
and
you are blessed,
addressed and known.

—Chaim Stern

Glory to thee, my God this night
for all the blessings of the light;
keep me, O keep me, King of kings,
beneath thine own almighty wings.

Forgive me, Lord, for thy dear Son,
the ill that I this day have done,
that with the world, myself, and thee,
I, ere I sleep, at peace may be.

—Thomas Ken (1637-1711), England

Heavenly Father, as I count your many blessings,
your gift of forgiveness is by far the most precious.
Please create in me a forgiving heart
that I might reveal your love and mercy.

—Catherine Coyle

Lord, let no unnecessary sense of guilt
prevent me from being used by Thee,
let not the knowledge of my unworthiness
prevent me from being used by Thee.
Lord, never let the forgiven past
prevent me from being used by Thee.
And may I this coming day
be able to do some work of peace for Thee.

—Alan Paton (1903-1988), South Africa

Without forgiveness there is no love.
Without love there is no growth.
Without growth there is no continuing life.

When in the Gospels Christ heals and forgives he also sends out.

Go, he says, and use your giftedness.
Go, now you are set free for mission.
Go, and live out fully the life that you have been given.

—Esther De Waal, England

May the God of gentleness, support, and sustaining love gather us in her arms this night and bless us with sleep that restores both body and soul. Amen

—Marchiene Vroon Rienstra

Repeating one breath prayer slowly, many times, allows its meaning to deepen in us. We experience the truth of the words and carry them with us wherever we go.

O God / giver of life,
bearer of pain / maker of love.

In your love and tenderness / remake me.

I will be still / and learn,
Spirit of peace / within me.

O God / save me from myself.

Blessed Jesus / I am broken.
Mend me. /
Heal me. /
Make me / whole.

O Love / no more sins!

Trust in / the slow work of God.

Set me free / to love.

Not my will / but yours be done.

God gives us grace / to forgive.

A new heart / I will give you.
A new spirit / I will put within you.

Lord, make me an instrument of your peace.
Where there is hatred, let me sow love.
Where there is injury, pardon.
Where there is discord, vision.
Where there is doubt, faith.
Where there is despair, hope.
Where there is darkness, light.
Where there is sadness, joy.
O divine Master,
grant that I may not so much seek to be consoled as to console;
to be understood as to understand;
to be loved, as to love;
for it is in giving that we receive,
it is in pardoning that we are pardoned,
and it is in dying that we are born to eternal life.

—anonymous, c. 1913, (commonly called the Prayer of St. Francis)

Chapter 2

Learning to Forgive

Be kind to one another, tenderhearted, forgiving one another as God in Christ forgave you.

—Ephesians 4:32

Put on then, as God's chosen ones, holy and beloved, compassion, kindness, lowliness, meekness, and patience, forbearing one another and, if one has a complaint against another, forgiving each other; as the Lord has forgiven you, so you also must forgive. And above all these put on love, which binds everything together in perfect harmony.

—Colossians 3:12-14

When the apostles asked Jesus to teach them how to pray, he responded with a prayer that is an entire school of prayer, an entire school of life. It is awesome. And it is frightening. Forgive us our trespasses as we forgive those who trespass against us. I have always hastened to add in my heart, "Lord, I forgive everyone as fully as I can."

—M. Basil Pennington

If you forgive someone's sins, they're gone for good. If you don't forgive sins, what are you going to do with them?

—paraphrase John 20:23, Eugene H. Peterson, *The Message*

Truth without love kills, but love without truth lies.

—Eberhard Arnold (1883-1935)

Forgiveness does not mean we suppress our anger . . . None of this, "I'm too spiritual to be angry," for who among us is? Rather, we pray, "I am angry, dear God. But I am willing not to be. I am willing to see this situation another way."

—Marianne Williamson

O my Lord—wash me,
wash me of this relationship;
wash me of the pain of it,
wash me of the hurt of it,
wash me of the disappointment of it,
wash me of the resentment of it,
wash me of the attachment to it,
wash me of the hurtful memories of it
that come back in quietness, and in prayer,
that come back in the silent night hours.

I give myself into your hands, Lord,
Do for me what I cannot do for myself.
Heal me, Lord.
Under your healing touch
hour by hour, and day by day
I shall be set free.

  —author unknown

✒

Lord, take away this cup of bitterness. Break my anger, as my heart has been broken.

 In the darkness of my hurt, let there be hope. And, one day, perhaps, let there be love again.

  —Jane Robson

Lord, this is what went wrong . . .
I give it all to you,
every detail, every barb, every frustration,
the major things and the petty things.
May the pain which I am feeling be for healing,
and not a spring of bitterness.
May my thoughts be Christ-centered,
and for those involved,
rather than self-centered
and against them.

—Angela Ashwin, England

L❦

Write the wrongs that are done to you in sand, but write the
good things that happen to you on a piece of marble. Let go of all
emotions such as resentment and retaliation, which diminish you,
and hold onto the emotions, such as gratitude and joy, which
increase you.

—Arabic proverb

*F*orgiveness, far from being merely another human activity, is the miraculous work of the Holy Spirit in us. What we can do is to ask constantly for this gift and not set up obstacles to its operation in our lives. If . . . the desire not to close the door to a new beginning . . . remains alive in us, God will see to it that forgiveness opens a way forward. The day will come when we realize that a situation which seemed frozen has been transfigured, in all likelihood without our knowing exactly how this came about.

—Letter from Taizé, 1999 no. 3

I really must digress to tell you a bit of good news. Last week, while at prayer, I suddenly discovered—or felt as if I did—that I had really forgiven someone I have been trying to forgive for over thirty years. Trying, and praying that I might. When the thing actually happened, my feeling was "But it's so easy. Why didn't you do it ages ago?" So many things are done easily the moment you can do them at all. But till then, sheerly impossible, like learning to swim. There are months during which no efforts will keep you up; then comes the day and hour and minute after which, and ever after, it becomes almost impossible to sink . . .

The important thing is that a discord has been resolved, and it is certainly the great Resolver who has done it.

—C.S. Lewis (1898-1963), England

Each time I think
I've learned to handle hurt
I find I'm facing even deeper need,
and somehow all the learning
that has gone before
no longer is enough,
except perhaps—
do I turn more quickly from myself,
my self-sufficiency,
to you?
Give me your strength, Lord.
I need it.

—Lois Walfrid Johnson

I think that in order to really have a forgiving sense . . . you need
to recognize in a humble way that you, too, have hurt people, and
you've been forgiven for some of those hurts. . . . As people reflect
on those times, they usually feel very grateful. They say, "I deserved
condemnation for this nasty thing I did, but I got forgiveness, and
I'm grateful—and I really would like to give that gift of freedom to
the person who hurt me."

—Everett L. Worthington, Jr.

Dear Lord, help me to release my need to control.
Help me to let go and to accept Your will.
I now place this situation lovingly into Your hands.
I pray for the highest and the best of all concerned.
Thank you, thank you, thank you. Amen

—Robert and Janet Ellsworth

God of tears and God of laughter . . .
Laughter has been missing in much of my life.
I have been afraid of laughter because of the many times I was ridiculed and mocked.
Help me to know that love and laughter can go together.
Help me to discover the joy and delight in laughter shared.
Forgive me for the times my fear has led me to laugh at others.
Forgive those who have mocked me in the past.
Teach them and me the gift of loving laughter.

—Jane Vennard

Give me this night, O God,
the peace of mind which is truly rest.
Take from me all envy of anyone else,
all resentment for anything which has been withheld from me,
all bitterness against anyone who has hurt or wronged me,
all anger against the apparent injustices of life,
all foolish worry about the future,
and all futile regret about the past.
Help me to be
at peace with myself,
at peace with my fellow human beings,
at peace with you.
So indeed may I lay myself down to rest in peace,
through Jesus Christ my Lord.

—author unknown

*A*bbot Pastor said: If a man has done wrong and does not deny it, but says: I did wrong, do not rebuke him, because you will break the resolution of his soul. If you tell him: Do not be sad, brother, but watch it in the future, you stir him up to change his life.

—Sayings of the Desert Fathers (second and third centuries)

*P*erhaps the most important thing we bring to another person is the silence in us. Not the sort of silence that is filled with unspoken criticism or hard withdrawal. The sort of silence that is a place of refuge, of rest, of acceptance of someone as they are. We are all hungry for this other silence. It is hard to find. In its presence we can remember something beyond the moment, a strength on which to build a life. Silence is a place of great power and healing. Silence is God's lap.

—Rachel Naomi Remen

In the name of the living Christ, I set you free from my resentment and my expectations. Go on your way in peace. Thanks be to God who sets us free.

—Flora Slosson Wuellner

🌿

To forgive for the moment is not difficult. But to go on forgiving, to forgive the same offense again every time it recurs to the memory—there's the real tussle.

—C.S. Lewis (1898-1963), England

*T*oday I choose to pray for others.
But how shall I impart to them
the gift of peace and love
if my own heart is still unloving
and I have no peace of mind myself?

So I start with my heart:
I hold before the Lord
each feeling of resentment, anger, bitterness . . .
that may still be lurking there,
asking that God's grace
will make it yield to love someday
if not right now.

Then I seek the depth that silence brings,
for prayer that springs from silence
is powerful and effective.
So I listen to the sounds around me . . .
or become aware of the sensations in my body . . .
or my breathing in and out . . .

First I pray for people whom I love.
Over each of them I say a blessing:
"May you be safe from harm and evil,"
imagining that my words create
a protective shield of grace around them.

I think of the young . . . and recite this prayer:
"May the promise of your youth be met
and your life be fruitful."

Then I move on to the people I dislike
and the people who dislike me.
Over each of them I say this prayer:
"May you and I be friends some day,"
imagining some future scene
where this comes to pass.

Finally I say to each of the people I care for:
"May my time with you be a grace for both of us."

I come back to my heart now to rest awhile
in the silence that I find there . . .
and in the love that has come alive in me
as a consequence of my prayer for others . . .

  —Anthony de Mello (1931-1987), India

*H*ealing requires that we reach out, not necessarily to those who have hurt us, but at least to something that gives us new life, new hope, new pleasure. Healing is the process of refusing to be wounded.

"Our greatest glory," Confucius wrote, "is not in never falling but in rising every time we fall." War against the war within the self by making peace with it early. Yes, we have been hurt; no, we will never trust the same situation again. But . . . we know more about life now than we did before and, when we are totally involved in something else, we are more than capable of dealing with it.

If the message we're supposed to be getting is really, "Forgive us . . . as we forgive" it's time to let everything to the mercy of God, to put down unholy righteousness, to purge ourselves of grudges and to move where we're welcome, uncaring of where we're not.

—Joan D. Chittister, OSB

Whatever harm I may have done
In all my life in all your wide creation
If I cannot repair it
I beg you to repair it,

And then there are all the wounded,
The poor the deaf the lonely and the old
Whom I have roughly dismissed
As if I were not one of them.
Where I have wronged them by it
And cannot make amends
I ask you
To comfort them to overflowing,

And where there are lives I may have withered around me,
Or lives of strangers far or near
That I've destroyed in blind complicity,
And if I cannot find them
Or have no way to serve them,

Remember them. I beg you to remember them

When winter is over
And all your unimaginable promises
Burst into song on death's bare branches.

—Anne Porter

O God of love, we pray thee to give us love:
love in our thinking, love in our speaking,
love in our doing, and love in the hidden places of our souls;
love of our neighbors near and far;
love of our friends, old and new;
love of those with whom we find it hard to bear,
and love of those who find it hard to bear with us;
love of those with whom we work,
and love of those with whom we take our ease;
love in joy, love in sorrow;
love in life and love in death;
that so at length we may be worthy to dwell in thee,
who art eternal love.

—William Temple (1881-1944), England

❧

O Great Spirit of Surprise,
dazzle us with a day full of amazing embraces,
capricious, uncalculated caring,
great hearts, kind souls, and doers of good deeds.

—Molly Fumia

*H*ow simple it is
this being alive
in the clearing which
openness brings.
This being alive among the boxes
tumbled among ourselves
boxes all windowed and door'd,
opening, closing
freeing and muffling
our angry shoutings, our singing
and our laughter.
This being alive in the
clearing where we
reach and withdraw
reach, touch, and withdraw
afraid and brave at once
to the possibilities of us.
How simple it is
this being alive
in the clearing which
openness brings.

—David Cysewski, "How Simple It Is"

Breath prayers can be prayed silently anywhere, whenever we remember a relationship or an inner attitude of our own that needs healing.

May the words spoken today / heal our hearts,
calm our concerns / and give us hope.

When I speak today / give me good speech.

Set a watch over my mouth / O Lord.

Show me the truth / of this situation.

Listening is healing. / Listening is love.

May I meet in mercy / all who seek me.

I bless / this situation.
I bless / this person.
God bless us / all of us.

May ____ look at me / with the eyes of a friend.
Let us see each other / with the eyes of friends.

Where fear paralyzes / let forgiveness break through.

God's loving presence / will be with us.

May the Lord / give you peace.

The past / is in the past.

Fear less, hope more;
eat less, chew more;
whine less, breathe more;
talk less, say more;
hate less, love more;
and all good things are yours.

—Old Swedish prayer

Celebrating a birthday is exalting life and being glad for it. On a birthday we do not say: "Thank you for what you did, or said, or accomplished." No, we say: "Thank you for being born and being among us." . . . Celebrating a birthday reminds us of the goodness of life, and in this spirit we really need to celebrate people's birthdays every day, by showing gratitude, kindness, forgiveness, gentleness, and affection. These are ways of saying: "It's good that you are alive; it's good that you are walking with me on this earth. Let's be glad and rejoice. This is the day that God has made for us to be and to be together."

—Henri J.M. Nouwen (1932-1996)

May the love of Christ continue to bind us together
in joy and sorrow,
through laughter and tears,
with love and hope
for years to come. Amen

—the Nilsen family

May you be filled with loving kindness.
May you be well.
May you be peaceful and at ease.
May you be happy.

—ancient Tibetan Buddhist blessing

May you be happy.
May you be free.
May you be loving.
May you be loved. . . .
May every fiber of your being resonate to the glory
    to which God calls you.
May you be successful in every endeavor.
May you experience the fullness of peace in body and soul.
May you know the Lord in all his goodness.
May you forgive every transgression.
I forgive you with all my heart and soul.
May you know what it means to be a child of God.
May you experience the glory of possessing the kingdom of God.
May you live and walk in peace and fellowship
    with all of God's creatures.
May every blessing be yours.
May goodness and love show itself in everything
    that you do and all that is done to you.
May you be one with all of God's creation.
May you experience the blessings of God's grace for all eternity!

—Father William A. Meninger

May the long time sun shine on you,
all love surround you,
and the pure light within you,
guide your way on.

—traditional Celtic farewell blessing

Chapter 3

Forgiving Ourselves

Jesus, I need healing.
At times I have a Judas voice
which betrays the Christ in me and others.
There is also a Pontius Pilate who will shrug
and walk away from the suffering in the world,
a Peter who panics and denies the truth.
Jesus, the scenes of your trial and crucifixion
get acted out in me, time after time,
and there are days when I find it hard
to look at myself in the mirror.
I need you to remind me
that forgiveness begins with self.
Life is a journey of contrasts.
It is light which makes shadows,
hills which cause valleys,
and it is your life in me
which makes me so aware
of the beauty and frailty of being human.
Jesus, show me how to be gentle
with myself, how to repair with love
the damage that I do to myself and others.
And in my moments of despair,
draw me back to your Easter message—
that there can be no resurrections
without crucifixions.

—Joy Cowley, New Zealand

Strength of the weary,
I argue with myself.
It was my fault.
No, I'm not to blame.
Yes, I am.
I could have done this.
I should have done that.
Maybe I just didn't try
hard enough
long enough.
And I sigh.
I can't relive the past, nor find a simple route
through the maze,
as if there is an easy answer
to what happened to us.
When I'm tired or prone to doubt
I blame myself—
the easy way out.
It is self-recrimination,
self destruction,
and it keeps me from going on.

  —Judith Mattison

*H*elp me, God, to know what is my fault and ask forgiveness; to know what is not mine and let it go.

—Mary Cabrini Durkin and Sheila Durkin Dierks

✎♥

*G*enuine guilt is an arousal of the heart, an alarm that warns us of a wound for which we are responsible. Such guilt is a gift, a gift that alerts us to an injured relationship—with a friend, with God, with our own best hopes and deepest values. False guilt lures us from a focus on what we have done to an absorption with how bad we are. The mood moves from "I have failed here" to "I am a failure." In this maelstrom of defeat, I lose sight of the particular behaviors that I can and should change. I even lose sight of the relationship that I have injured. Increasingly, the focus is on me—my wretchedness, my failure, my pain . . . I give this disruptive mood power over me. The gift of guilt becomes a curse, and reconciliation escapes me.

—George S. Johnson

*A*ccept me, O Lord, just as I am,
in my frailty, my inadequacy, my contradictions and my confusions.
Accept me, with all those discordant currents
that pull me in so many directions.
Accept all of this, and help me so to live with what I am,
that what I am may become my way to you.

　　—based on the "Suscipe me," a prayer made by a novice on
entering a Benedictine community

Dear God, I need to see myself as you see me.
My own vision is fragmented.
I try to divide up my life
and reject those parts of me I consider to be weak.
I waste time and energy in the battle of self against self
and Lord, I always end up the loser.

Dear God, help me to see myself as you see me.
I forget that you made me just as I am
and that you delight in your creation.
You do not ask me to be strong;
you simply ask me to be yours.
You do not expect me to reject my weakness,
merely to surrender it to your healing touch.

Dear God, when I can see myself as you see me,
then I will understand that this frail, tender, fearful, aching,
singing, half-empty, shining, shadowed person
is a whole being made especially by you for your love.

—Joy Cowley, New Zealand

Don't carry on a futile battle against yourself, don't divide yourself into good and evil.

Resist the temptation to analyze yourself—turn your attention to the Lord instead, and be deeply receptive.

Accept yourself in God's light and concentrate on the mission you have to accomplish.

—anonymous

Grace strikes us when we are in great pain and restlessness. It strikes us when we walk through the dark valley of a meaningless and empty life. It strikes us when our disgust for our own being, our indifference, our weakness, our hostility, and our lack of direction and composure have become intolerable to us. It strikes us when, year after year, the longed-for perfection of life does not appear, when the old compulsions reign within us as they have for decades, when despair destroys all joy and courage. Sometimes at that moment a wave of light breaks into our darkness, and it is as though a voice were saying: "You are accepted."

—Paul Tillich (1886-1965)

Perhaps I am not so much a person,
as the raw materials for a person,
and my life is the time of creation.

Perhaps every part of me has a value,
even the parts I despise;
and each has a crucial role to play in the story of my existence.

Creator of the Universe,
fount of things strange and wonderful,
Praise to you for the mystery of my being.

Help me put myself together.

Out of all the notes that play in me,
even those that sound harsh now,
help me to make a symphony both of us can enjoy.

—Kathleen Fischer and Thomas Hart

I am glad for all the good that is in me, while I struggle against what is not.

—Robert A. Raines

Be patient with everyone, but above all with yourself . . . do not be disheartened by your imperfections, but always rise up with fresh courage. How are we to be patient in dealing with our neighbor's faults if we are impatient in dealing with our own? They who are fretted by their own failings will not correct them. All profitable correction comes from a calm and peaceful mind.

—Saint Francis de Sales (1567-1622), France

We need to remember that even as new persons in a new creation, we will still feel some sorrow whether we are the injured or an injurer. Harm has been done, and the bodily or emotional damage in this life may be permanent. This mature, genuine sorrow should not be confused with nonforgiveness either of others or of ourselves. This sorrow is the aching of old scar tissue. Jesus' wounds on his risen body after Easter had become sources and signs of transformation and healing for others. Nevertheless, they were still wound marks. Pain and sorrow are never wasted when given into God's hands, and their transformation is far beyond our imaginings. But in this life, we will experience a poignancy, a regret that harm was done when our actions could have been different. This poignancy is a valid, healthy part of our journey of release.

—Flora Slosson Wuellner

Breath prayers can be used to help forgive yourself, to have mercy on yourself, to allow yourself to be forgiven and healed.

God is greater / than my heart.

Lord / you have forgiven me.
Help me / to forgive myself.

Make me able / to welcome your love.

I ask for courage / to accept my failures.
I ask for peace / to let them go.

I am much more / than my mistakes.

I give you thanks / for the gift of my life.

This day / can be a new beginning.

When change comes slowly / may I be patient.

God loves me. / God forgives me.

I am loved. / I am forgiven.

You are precious in my sight / and I love you.

Spirit of Hope, blessed be this new life.
Blessed be this new beginning.
Blessed be this healing.
Blessed be this letting go, and this keeping.
Spirit of Hope, blessed be this new life.

—author unknown

✑

Dear God, I love myself for what I'm gonna be some day. I will be someone, somebody soon. When I get strong. I love you.

—Dolores, a recovering alcoholic and prostitute

We strengthen life anytime that we listen generously or encourage someone to find meaning, or wonder about possibility, or dream or hope for escape from self-judgment and inner criticism, or know that they matter. Anytime we share someone's joy, we bless the life in them.

—Rachel Naomi Remen

This truth I firmly hold, all evidence to the contrary not withstanding: My life has been a gift, a blessing to the world.

—Anthony de Mello (1931-1987), India

Chapter 4

Loving Family and Friends

Dear God, please bless my parents.
Thank you, thank them for the life they gave me.
For the ways they helped me and made me strong, I give thanks.
For the ways they stumbled and held me back,
please help me to forgive them and receive Your compensation.
May their spirits be blessed, their roads forward made easy.
Please release them, and release me, from my childhood now gone by.
Release us also from any bitterness I still hold.
They paved the way, in all that they did,
for where I have been has led me here.
I surrender my parents to the arms of God.
Thank you, dear ones, for your service to me.
Bless your souls.
May your spirits fly free.
May we enter into the relationship God wills for us.
Thank You, Lord, for I am free now.
Glory, hallelujah. Amen

—Marianne Williamson

My father had such high expectations for me. He wanted for me a life that he had dreamed about. But he was not a man to display affection. He never told me that he loved me. When he lost his patience with me, he could be overbearing. There were times he whipped me when a word would have been sufficient. And "I'm sorry" wasn't in his vocabulary.

For a long time, I held a grudge about that. I needed to hear him tell me that he loved me. He told my sister he loved her, so why couldn't he say that to me?

Well, I decided two can play that game. So I stopped telling him that I loved him. Stubbornness seemed to run in the family. Like father, like son. So both of us let years pass without using the word love. Oh, we shook hands formally. But he shook hands with everyone.

As his condition deteriorated I realized that he . . . wasn't going to change. If changing was to be done, I had to do it.

If I had been assured that as soon as I said, "I love you," he would say something like, "Well, I love you, too," it would have been so much easier. But he didn't. At least, not for a long time.

It took so much time, but the gap between us had been narrowed and was narrowing. I think that with a little more time, we both could have reached out and touched hands and found no gap at all.

Perhaps the narrowing we accomplished was enough of a miracle.

—Harold Ivan Smith

A wise friend told me that she experiences her father as a better dad now than when he was alive, because she knows that now he sees her through Jesus' eyes. He sees when he hurt her, and knows he is forgiven. He looks back on times when she hurt him and can forgive, because now, like our Lord, he understands why.

I remember one time asking a therapist how I was going to cope with my parents' deaths, since the alienation seemed so entrenched and inevitable. She said I would grieve twice—once for the parent I lost, and once for the parent I never had. But she didn't tell me about the grace of having a father finally become the parent he could never be in this life.

Today I feel loved, protected, and cherished. . . . I think of my parents now as "The Ones Who Know the Whole Story."

—Barbara Allen

Be my mother tonight, O God,
because my mother died this afternoon.
Our close moments came only when we fought;
I never confided in her or made her my friend;
we didn't laugh at the same moment or exchange glances
across a room, the way my daughters and I do.
I was angry at her a lot, and she at me.
She wasn't wise. But she was my mother,
and I loved her and now I don't have her.
I think maybe you've been my mother all my life, God.
Stay close, please, I need you tonight. Amen

—Kristen Johnson Ingram

All those old jokes about mothers-in-law were never
very funny to me.
The first day we met,
you took one look at me
and decided you didn't like me,
and you never really changed your mind.
I wasn't good enough for your daughter,
and I never would be.
Your rejection hurt,
and I have to admit that sometimes it still does.
But even more painful was your criticism
of my wife—your daughter—
and our children.
You and I survived mainly by staying out of one another's way.
It wasn't good,
but neither of us knew how to do any better.
God knows I wasn't able to love you
any more than you were able to love me.
Maybe we each gave the other what we could,
and that has to be enough.
I'm trying to forgive you,
not because you need to receive forgiveness,
but because I need to offer it.
Maybe God, who can do more than we can imagine,
can still open the way to reconciliation between us.
I hope so.
I hope you do too.

—Ron Klug, "To My Mother-in-Law, Deceased"

I was born to be
an evening primrose.
I was destined to
blossom into
a poet
a writer
a musician
an artist
a teacher and
healer
but my family
wrapped itself tightly
around my tender fragile petals
binding and restraining me . . .
and I have never blossomed.
O God, be with me, as I try to bloom.

—anonymous

I lie in bed as if with a stranger. He's awake, but we don't speak, and I take pains not to touch him. Hard and brittle, I could easily shatter. I am hurt and angry, deeply disappointed and, oh God, I have never felt so alone.

I hear his muffled breathing, breath you have given, God, and a bit of sympathy leaks out. I love him so much. Otherwise, why would it hurt? You love this man, too. You have a plan for him. I huddle on my edge of the bed, longing to be wrapped once again in warmth and intimacy. What does this mean for us?

This place hurts, but I can survive it. When I call, you will come. You are a cool hand on my forehead, a cleansing river that sweeps away fear. You gather up all our longing in your arms and bless it. Away across the sheets lies one who you also call by name. Giver of all good things, grant us rest this night. In the morning may we turn our faces toward you—and each other—and move forward one step at a time.

—anonymous

I'm hurt and I'm angry
and I'm using silence
as both shield and weapon.
So is my partner.
I don't know what else to do.
I'm afraid if I say anything,
I'll only cause more hurt
to my partner or myself.

But I know that silence is the enemy of peace.
So make me strong enough to say the first word.
And even though what I say is not perfect,
please let them be healing words.

—Ron Klug

Sometimes it's hard to tell someone to her face, I love you.
Sometimes it's easier to say, go to hell,
and slam the door.

Lord, unslam my door so she can come in
and I can go out . . .
unstop my ears so I can hear her sighs and songs
and my own . . .
unblind my eyes so I can see the lonely human being in her anger
and hurt
and my own . . .

and, free me
to tell her to her face,
I love you.

—Robert A. Raines

Too often I wait with building memories
until they must of necessity become memorials.
Help me, Lord, to create moments of joy or tenderness,
laughter or silence, listening or sharing my heart—
moments as valued as drops of dew because they vanish as quickly.
Help me, Lord, to create moments that live on
when the person I love is home with you.

—Lois Walfrid Johnson

We have lost contact again—
a husband and wife
who love and live
together—
sit, speak, eat, sleep
together—
we have disconnected ourselves
and left each other alone.

We push words at each other,
but there is no response.
We eat our food together
for the sake of habit and health,
but there is no communion.
We perform our duties and services
for those who depend on our activity,
but there is no blessing.
We give ourselves to each other,
and even this is—a complaint,
and it is difficult to sleep.

Lord Jesus Christ,
forgive my foolishness,
my pride, my silence.

I will go to him now and touch him.
I will put my hand in his,
and I will say the difficult words,
"Forgive me," and, "I forgive you."

I need love to do this, Lord Jesus,
the kind of love You give me.

—Anne Springsteen

O God, out of all the world you let us find one another and learn together the meaning of love. Let us never fail to hold love precious. Let the flame of it never waver or grow dim, but burn in our hearts as an unwavering devotion and shine through our eyes in gentleness and understanding on which no shadow falls. . . .

Teach us to remember the little courtesies, to be swift to speak the grateful and happy word, to believe rejoicingly in each other's best, and to face all life bravely because we face it with united hearts.

—Walter Russell Bowie (1882-1969)

$\mathcal{L}$❤

At some moment, we must say it was a failure.
We were not able to care enough, to understand adequately.
I have said and done things which hurt you or did not try to help.
I have ignored or raged or kept my feelings to myself.
We did not do our best.
It is not a sign that we should go on together.
It is simply an acknowledgment that we have sinned.

—Judith Mattison

Lord, to whom shall I go? My marriage has failed, and I must share the blame. We were not good for each other or to each other. Finally, my silent voice had to scream, "No." And in the leaving there has been more hurt —my children, my parents, my colleagues, my friends, even my ex, who would rather choose death in the marriage than life outside the marriage. My heart aches for the pain I've known and the pain I've caused. Forgive me, Jesus, and help me to forgive the others. Release me from anger, guilt, and shame. Heal my weary soul. Give me sight to see that you, Lord, have the words of eternal life—words of love and forgiveness. Amen

—Roberta French

Sometimes I can't find words
to tell my loved ones
how much they mean to me
or what's important.
So I keep still,
my hopes,
fears,

needs,
thanks,
bottled inside.

Is that why others too keep still?
Lord, we need each other.
Please help us see communication

as an act of faith—
faith in you
and in each other.

  —Catharine Brandt

Well, I've burned the beans again,
and I'd like to throw the pot and all
right through the window.

Christ, forgive me.

Sometime between breakfast and lunch
I grabbed the day by the throat—
apparently I intended to kill it
before it got me
and I almost succeeded.
I forgot that it was Your day.

Christ, have mercy on me.
Forgive me.

I really don't care too much about the beans.
I can save enough to put on the table.
But I have nearly destroyed one whole day!
I have carelessly burned some people —
the ones with whom I will now sit down to eat.

Christ, forgive me and help me.

There are still a few hours left.
Be present at our table Lord.
Let this supper be joyful for us
because we ask and receive Your blessing.

  —Anne Springsteen

*H*owever unacceptable the package, there's always a Holy Miracle inside: inside the surly teenager sitting coldly across from me at dinner is a confused little boy yearning to become someone he's not, and too afraid to risk being who he is. Inside the angry mother yelling at her crying child in the supermarket is an overwhelmed woman, herself a crying child, bone-tired and bone-lonely.

My heart, no stranger to suffering, can easily cross the bridge to another suffering heart, when I get my judgments out of the way.

—Sheila Morgan

*A*s I kneel to pray, the sun is setting. There are but minutes left in the day. Give me the courage to go in haste and say to my friend, "I am angry and we must talk. But first, be assured that I love you." Amen

—Scott Walker

She's seated in her no-longer-thick-plush green chair,
    which rocks a little bit.
This is her chair.
Even the children feel strange rocking in it
    after Grandma goes to bed.
She's not looking at me.
This is her chair, and when she sits in it,
if she's not reading or watching the news,
she looks down the hallway.
Her hands are quiet.

We're close enough to stub each other's toe.
We're so far apart I send messenger pigeons to find her.
A lot of birds peter out halfway.
Others fly right past her.
A surprising number of pigeons are actually shot down.
A precious few land
are welcomed
and sent back in a crafty smile.

    —L. Anderson, "I Try to Talk with My Mother-in-Law"

She doesn't know God forgives her. That's the only power you have—to tell her that. Not just that he forgives her the poor little adultery. But the faces she can't bear to look at now. The man's. Her husband's. Her own, half the time. Tell her he forgives her for being lonely and bored, for not being full of joy with a house full of children. That's what sin really is. You know—not being full of joy. Tell her that sin is forgiven because whether she knows it or not, that's what she wants more than anything else—what all of us want.

—Frederick Buechner

☙

Let the words of my mouth and the meditation of my heart be acceptable in thy sight.
You who created me, and all my wonderful parts, open my mouth.

I appear to be speaking, but I am not.
I'm making my mouth move,
and sounds come out, but they are not real.
I'm hiding what I really need to say
behind meaningless words.

I do not say:
I'm mad at you.
You hurt my feelings when you said that.
I feel jealous of you.

I say instead:
Everything's fine.
I'm just too busy to get together.
No! There's no problem!

I lie by omission, and the pain festers,
the alienation grows.
This gives me a sad kind of power,
because if the other person doesn't know anything is wrong,
they never get the opportunity to fix it.
They have to be the bad person,
and I get to be the silent sufferer.
Deep down I know that's not fair, or honest, or right.
It's just an easy way out for a coward like me.
Don't let me get away with this.
Give me courage.
Give me resolve.
Open my mouth.

     —Karen Batdorf

O God, this is one of the worst days of my life! I had to call in eight members of my team and tell them their positions were being cut, they were being downsized, let go, fired. I feel like a murderer. These were friends as well as colleagues. I hired some of them. Nearly all of them had been working as hard as they could, even putting in extra hours without extra pay. They didn't deserve this. Most of them have families to support. Some are middle-aged and will have a hard time finding another position. The job market is tight. They served the company well for years, and now they're being tossed aside like obsolete computers. They're hurt and they're afraid.

Forgive me, Lord, for what I did to them. I didn't want to do it. I had no choice. I thought about resigning, but that wouldn't help the ones who are leaving, and it would probably make things worse for those who remain. As it is, I'll now be asking each of them to do the work of two people. Still, I do blame myself. If I had been a better manager, maybe this wouldn't have happened. But I did the best I could.

If it's possible, let them forgive me and remember that I cared about them. Help them to move on. I will remember the pain in their faces for a long time. Help me move on. I'm scared. If we don't turn this company around, I'll be the next to go.

There must be a better way to do business than this. Lord help us find it.

—Martin Noll, "Prayer of a Corporate Manager"

"Forgive and forget," they say.
Well, Lord, as I grow older,
the forgetting part keeps getting easier.
But I'm not so sure about the forgiving.
Sometimes I get so irritated
over little things that would never have bothered me before.
I'm afraid I'm getting more intolerant and critical,
especially of young people, even my own family.
I'm finding it harder to let go of grudges.
Lord, I don't want to become a crotchety, crabby senior citizen!
I'd like it if you could make me more forgetful
of my aches and pains and the little irritations of each day.
Keep me growing and mindful of others, and useful where I live.
Thank you that your world is a beautiful and fascinating place,
filled with wonderful people
who still need me.

—Paul Nieman

Lord, there are two frustrations to my disability.
First the physical limitations,
but second the way people's attitudes to those limitations
poison their relationships with me.
Please help me to forgive them.

It feels painful that so many people now see me
in terms of what I cannot do,
or in terms of what I do differently,
rather than as the person I am.

Being inside this crippled body feels like
being on the inside of a two-way mirror,
able to look out and see the "normal" people,
but without their awareness that I am on the other side.

When they look at me and into the mirror from their side
they see not me,
but a reflection of themselves in my situation.
It is as if they have accidentally walked into a hall of mirrors
at a fun-fair and been suddenly shocked
by a grotesquely distorted image of themselves,
of their plans, their hopes . . . their futures.

This instinctive reaction is clear in their faces when they meet me,
or look at me from across the street or park.
If they don't look away and are forced to come nearer,
the more obvious this fear of me becomes.
Because it is fear they are feeling.
They are afraid of the same thing happening to them.

So, Lord,
please help me to forgive the way they react to me
because I find it so difficult.
And, Lord,
please forgive me too,
because before I became disabled, I know
that I reacted to disabled people in just the same way.

—Peter Lockwood

Ok, so Lord . . . here's the deal:
I get sad and frightened and stupid and incompetent once in a while.
Right now, for instance.
I know it doesn't last.
I know I will feel better soon.
I know it's all in my hormones and synapses and brain chemistry.
I know that at times like this I believe lies about myself and
everybody else . . .
and I have trouble believing in You . . .
except that then the angels gather.
It scares me how they gather.
Someone writes.
Someone calls.
Someone brings me an extra grocery bag for my flowers so they
don't freeze before I get them in the car.
Someone rents a funny movie for me.
Someone understands how I feel and demands my best work anyway.

Someone keeps loving me no matter what.
The evidence all points to You being right there helping me through it
so that maybe I can be smart and happy next week.
I'm grateful. I am.
But, Jesus, I've been working so hard to love my family
and do my job and my music
and not let anybody down who depends on me.
I'm not only sad and frightened and stupid and incompetent . . .
I'm also really really really tired.
I'm sorry.
Help.

    —Holly Jo Turnquist Fischer

Lord, I bring before you
the needs of my parents, friends,
brothers, sister, all whom I love,
and all who have asked me to pray for them.
I pray that they may experience your help
and the gift of your comfort,
protection from all dangers,
deliverance from all sin,
and freedom from pain.
May they give you joyful thanks and praise.
I also bring before you
all those who have in any way
offended or insulted me,
or done me any harm.
I also remember those
whom I have hurt or offended or troubled
by what I said or did
knowingly or unknowingly.
Lord, in your mercy, forgive all our sins against one another.
Take from our hearts
all suspicion, hard feelings,
anger, dissension,
and whatever else may diminish the love
we could have for one another.
Have mercy, O Lord, on all who ask your mercy.
Give grace to all who need it,
that we may finally come to eternal life.

—Thomas á Kempis (1380-1471), Germany

In the night I am wide awake. A tiny change of plans has grown into a grandiose worry. I am doubting a good friend. I whisper my anger, my resentment. I think of things to say, to write, to do, to get even. I am angry against my friend and I cannot sleep.

Then I pray for other thoughts, for memories. I think of old times, good times, good feelings, a good friend. In the night I begin to make up with my friend. I think on our friendship, on a person I have long trusted. I remember laughter, the good times. I smile in the night. I know there is a good reason for the change of plans. I will ask; I will trust the friendship.

In the night a friendship can grow. Good feelings and thoughts soon turn to blessing, calm, prayer. In the night watch I thank God for my friend.

—Herb Brokering

Whenever you think of someone you want to forgive, bless, or reconcile with, breathe a simple prayer. Choose one of these or create your own. This kind of simple, repetitive prayer can be especially calming during the night.

Peace / be in this house.
Peace to this house / and to all who live here.

I want a home / where love can be found.

Be good to myself. / Be good to those around me.

Bring us closer to you / and to each other.

Hold me, comfort me, / bless me.
Hold my husband, / comfort him, bless him.
Hold us both / in your loving arms.

You are bone of my bone / and flesh of my flesh.

Jesus, be the bridge / between the love _____ needs
and the love / I can give.

I give thanks for _____ / who blesses my life.

Gently I hold _____ / in loving silence.

Lord, help me see _____ / as you do.

I am willing to forgive / and ask forgiveness.

Forgive everything. / Remember the best.

May the pain of regret / become the joy of forgiveness.

The choice to love / is open till we die.

*O*h, the comfort—the inexpressible comfort of feeling safe with a person—having neither to weigh thoughts nor measure words, but pouring them all right out, just as they are, chaff and grain together; certain that a faithful hand will take and sift them, keep what is worth keeping, and then with the breath of kindness blow the rest away.

—Dinah Maria Mulock Craik, England

*B*eauty of friendship grow between us,
friendship without guile, without malice, without striving.

Goodness of friendship grow between us,
friendship with light, with wings, with soul sharing.

Be in the eye of each friend of my journey
to bless and teach each one.

The eye of the Father be upon us,
the eye of the Son be upon us,
the eye of the Spirit be upon us,
the eye of the Friendly Three
be upon us forever.

—traditional Celtic blessing, (c. 450–c. 700)

Peace between neighbors,
peace between kindred,
peace between lovers,
in love of the King of Life.

Peace between person and person,
peace between wife and husband,
peace between parents and children,
the peace of Christ above all peace.

Bless, O Christ, my face,
let my face bless every thing;
bless, O Christ, mine eye,
let mine eye bless all it sees.

      —traditional Celtic blessing, (c. 450–c. 700)

Chapter 5

Loving Our Enemies

You have heard that it was said, "You shall love your neighbor and hate your enemy." But I say to you, Love your enemies and pray for those who persecute you, so that you may be children of your Father in heaven; for he makes his sun rise on the evil and on the good, and sends rain on the righteous and on the unrighteous.

—Matthew 5:43-45

If your heart is hardened against your enemy, and you are filled with anger and despair, turn to God with your feelings of abandonment, your desire for vengeance, your need for protection and deliverance. Give voice to these prayers as long as you must. God will not leave you there. God will soften your heart and fill you with compassion. Jesus' words, "Pray for those who persecute you," are as much a promise as they are a command.

—Jane Vennard

Pray for your enemies, that they may be holy and that all may be well with them. And should you think this is not serving God, rest assured that more than all prayers, this is indeed the service of God.

—The Talmud

Almighty and tender Lord Jesus Christ,
just as I have asked you to love my friends
So I ask the same for my enemies . . .
Whatever you make me desire for my enemies,
Give it to them.
And give the same back to me.
If I ever ask for them anything
which is outside your perfect rule of love,
whether through weakness, ignorance, or malice,
Good Lord, do not give it to them
and do not give it back to me.
You who are the true light, lighten their darkness.
You who are the whole truth, correct their errors.
You who are the incarnate word, give life to their souls . . .
Let them be reconciled with you,
and through you reconciled to me.

—Anselm of Canterbury (1033-1109), England

Bless those who persecute you; bless and do not curse them. Rejoice with those who rejoice, weep with those who weep. Live in harmony with one another; do not be haughty, but associate with the lowly . . . Do not pay anyone evil for evil, but take thought for what is noble in the sight of all. If it is possible, so far as it depends upon you, live peaceably with all. Beloved, never avenge yourselves, but leave room for the wrath of God; for it is written, "'Vengeance is mine, I will repay,' says the Lord." No, if your enemies are hungry, feed them; if they are thirsty, give them something to drink; for by doing this you will heap burning coals on their heads. Do not be overcome by evil, but overcome evil with good.

—Romans 12:14-21

Forgiveness is and always has been an impractical, illogical and uncommon approach to life: forgiving our enemies, doing good to those who hurt us, repaying evil with kindness. Contrary to myth, forgiveness is not instinctive, and most of the time it is a very difficult and time-consuming enterprise.

—Doris Donnelly

*H*atred is not diminished by hatred at any time.
Hatred is diminished by love.
This is an eternal law.

—Buddhist teaching

A brother asked one of the elders: What is humility? The elder
answered him: To do good to those who do evil to you. The brother
asked: Supposing a man cannot go that far, what should he do? The
elder replied: Let him get away from them and keep his mouth shut.

—Sayings of the Desert Fathers

I heard him say, Love your enemy.
And I thought, well, I did.
Sort of. From a distance.
As long as I don't have to talk to her
or share the same room for any time.
It wasn't that I hated her.
It was just a matter of principle.
I had to let her know
that I didn't approve.

But he kept saying, Love your enemy.
Over and over, Love your enemy.
And I thought, well, maybe
a bit closer wouldn't hurt.
A telephone call. Good morning.
Some questions of polite interest.
No need to compromise principles.
I could let her know
that I held no grudge.

He still kept saying it.
Love your enemy. Love your enemy.
So in the end, I had to go the whole hog.
Suddenly there we were, talking about feelings,
laughing and crying and hugging each other.
And I was healed of the wound I'd given myself
with my judgmental attitudes.

So the next time he said, Love your enemy,
I knew clearly what he meant.
My real enemy
is self.
And I need all the love and forgiveness
I can get.

  —Joy Cowley, New Zealand

Loving my enemies does not apparently mean thinking them nice. . . . That is an enormous relief. For a good many people imagine that forgiving your enemies means making out that they are really not such bad fellows after all, when it is quite plain that they are. Go a step further. In my most clear-sighted moments not only do I not think myself a nice man, but I know that I am a very nasty one. I can look at some of the things I have done with loathing and horror. So apparently I am allowed to loathe and hate some of the things my enemies do. Now that I come to think of it, I remember Christian teachers telling me long ago that I must hate a bad man's actions, but not hate the bad man: or as they would say, hate the sin but not the sinner. For a long time I used to think this is a silly straw-splitting distinction: how could you hate what a man did and not hate the man? But years later it occurred to me that there was one man to whom I had been doing this all my life—namely myself. However much I might dislike my own cowardice or conceit or greed, I went on loving myself. There had never been the slightest difficulty about it. In fact, the very reason why I hated the things was that I loved the man. Just because I loved myself I was sorry to find that I was the sort of man who did those things. Consequently Christianity does not want us to reduce by one atom the hatred we feel for cruelty and treachery. We ought to hate them. Not one word of what we have said about them needs to be unsaid. But it does want us to hate them in the same way in which we hate things in ourselves: being sorry that the man should have done such things, and hoping if it is any way possible, that somehow, sometime, somewhere, he can be cured and made human again.

—C.S. Lewis (1898-1963), England

Long enough, Yahweh—you've ignored me long enough.
I've looked at the back of your head long enough.
Long enough I've carried this ton of trouble,
lived with a stomach full of pain.
Long enough my arrogant enemies have
looked down their noses at me.

Take a good look at me, Yahweh, my God;
I want to look life in the eye,
so no enemy can get the best of me
or laugh when I fall on my face.

I've thrown myself headlong into your arms—
I'm celebrating your rescue.
I'm singing at the top of my lungs,
I'm so full of answered prayers.

   —paraphrase Psalm 13, Eugene H. Peterson, *The Message*

Take three deep breaths, focusing on the breath as it comes into and goes out of your body. In/Out.

When we are meeting opposition or hostility, deep breathing calms the mind and body, and turns us to God, who is love. Add any of the following phrases, or create you own, as you breathe. Or continue to pray without words.

O God / stay near.
Bless me / with your love.

I celebrate life in _____ / as well as in myself.

Forgive my enemies / and turn their hearts.

I forgive my enemy / at this moment
I open my heart / in forgiveness.

God can bring good / out of this.

Let us not / forget one another
but remember / and forgive.

Victory endures / when no one is defeated.

May the love of goodness / grow in _____.
May the love of goodness / grow in me.

In the midst of conflict / I am at peace.

God of power and might / shield and protect me.

May God bless us with love which overwhelms all hurt and anger, and grace which establishes all our good work. Amen

—Marchiene Vroon Rienstra

This soul did little good to me, O Lord,
but this soul was yours.

So to this soul I say:
I bless the day you were born,
I bless your growing up,
I bless you, even in your dark deeds,
and I bless you, soul, at your end.

Travel to the God who transforms.
Travel to the Arms so wide.
Travel to the Spirit all generous.

—traditional Celtic blessing, adapted by Ray Simpson

Chapter 6

Healing the Broken

O God, can't you do anything
for your wounded ones who walk the earth
in mournful resignation?
We are the ones who carry our burdens in silence.
We wear the masks of everyday politeness,
trying bravely to hold back the tears that so readily come.
We walk in loneliness,
not wanting to mar the joyful lives of others.
We are the ones who cry in the night,
the ones whose hearts pound, whose stomachs knot,
whose heads split in pain.
We are the ones who are paralyzed by fear or shame.
We are the ones who walk around with our lives in upheaval,
hoping against hope that the worst will not come.
We are the ones who kneel before you now
to pray for your mercy.

Can't you do anything for us?
Couldn't you at least take care of a few of us?
We would be grateful,
for we have compassion for one another.

You are our God; we learned mercy from you.
Wrap your arms about your wounded ones.
O God, our God, keep us from harm,
for we walk each day
in the hope of your healing mercy.

> —Ann Weems, "Lament Psalm Forty-one"

Once I took a broken toy
to my dad. Walked right up to him
toy in hand.
Looked up at him,
reaching out.
"Can you fix it?"
He carefully set aside his vodka and orange juice.
He stumbled slightly, eyes unfocused,
as he reached for my offering.
He took my small defenseless toy.
He worked to fix it, drunken hands
breaking it beyond repair.
When I tried to rescue it,
he pushed me away.
And I could do nothing to protect, to save
my fragile, broken toy.
God, at times my life feels broken.
I bring this fragile life to you.
Walk right up to you, life in hand.
Can we fix it?
I hold my breath and wait to see what you will do.

—Catherine J. Foote

Loving God, at this time my hurt is so deep and my heart is so devastated with pain that I cannot even begin to forgive this person. It is enough for now to know that my wounder is in your hands, even as I am, and with you there is perfect understanding and recompense for all my pain. When the time is right, help me to begin my journey of healing and release.

—Flora Slosson Wuellner

You are precious in God's sight. That is the thought to hold on to for however many hours, days, weeks, months, or years it takes to come to terms with the experience of being attacked or robbed. You are precious in God's sight. Don't try to dredge up feelings of love or forgiveness for your attacker or for the violator of your home and possessions, but concentrate on your own inner rehabilitation before God. You are precious. You have been wounded, whether physically or emotionally or through losing your possessions, and you need time for that wound to heal to a mere scar. Till then, prayer will be interrupted by flashbacks and lack of concentration, but you are precious in God's sight.

—Linette Martin, England

What is the language spoken here?
This is the language of truth.
To say what really happened, to talk about how I really feel.
No veiled references, no covered up words,
but to say this happened, this happened; to tell myself the truth.
What is the language spoken here?
I hear the words of truth.
True emotion, anger, loss.
He hurt me, she left me.
They were too scared, they scared me.
I look for a place where I can hear the words of my native tongue.
I have been a stranger in their midst too long.
Now I speak the language of truth.
The choking in my throat screams truth,
the aching in my soul insists on truth.
Now I speak my native tongue.
Here I tell the truth. Amen

—Catherine J. Foote

Heal the broken
with comforting words of God.
Cheer them gently
with earthly joys.
Be merry and laugh
with the broken
and carry their secret needs
in the deepest silence of your heart.

—Mechtild of Magdeburg (1210-1280), Germany

O God, our comforter in hard times, often have we called to you
in pain and you have answered our pleas. Here we sit this night,
guardians of a shelter where women lie sleeping, briefly safe from
the battering and bitterness of a world that does not protect them.
They look to us to knit together their shattered hopes, dreams, and
lives. But you, O God, are the tailor, the binder of wounds, and the
great healer. Help us to be conduits for your love, to reveal you to
them, and in seeing their joy, to know you more deeply. In the
name of him who fully opened himself to all in need, Jesus Christ,
your Son. Amen

—The Reverend Jayne Oasin

A woman enrolled in one of my classes while she was in the midst of a trial as the victim of a rapist. I suggested that she might want to wait to take the course, as discussions on sin and forgiveness would undoubtedly open wounds for her, but she wanted to stay.

One time after we came to the session in class on loving enemies, she came to my office and said, "You know, that sounds good, and I know that Jesus said it, but I want the guy to rot in hell." I told her that I understood that. She then asked, "You talked about people praying. What did you mean?"

I answered by asking, "Would you be willing to let me pray for him for you?" There was a long silence. Then she said, "Well, I suppose."

A couple of months went by. She stopped me one day on campus and said, "Are you praying for him?" I said yes. She said, "O.K."

Six more months went by, and she came by my office. She asked, "Are you still praying for him?" I said yes, and she said, "Yes, I am too." I asked her what she was praying, and she said, "I don't know. I just call out his name."

Two years later she wrote me a letter and said that she still could only call out his name. "But," she added, "I hope you are still praying for him."

Forgiveness can take a long time. A very long time.

—L. Gregory Jones

Loving God, I know that you hold me in the palm of your hand.
I know it is so.
But why, O Lord, why?
I rage at this sin against me, at this defilement of my body,
this assault on my peace of mind.

I mourn my lost serenity, security, confidence;
I mourn the loss of my ease and open nature.
I hate what his assault has done to me.
I feel that my body and soul may never be the same.
What has been forced upon me may not be forgotten.

But send your healing upon me like cool rain.
Soothe my spirit with the balm of your tender love.
Help me to feel secure again, as safe as ever within the shelter
of the Lord.

Let my anger not turn inward to self-loathing,
but outward for action and purpose: to help others like me,
to bring hope to those whose faith is not so strong.
Help me, with your grace,
to move beyond victim, to call myself survivor instead.

May you forgive this man's offense against me,
and grant me the peace and serenity
of a mind and body made whole again. Amen

——Julia Park

I am not a successful overcomer, Lord. I don't know if that needs forgiving or not.

Everywhere I look there are heart-warming stories of other people who have overcome enormous difficulties, who say yes, they were depressed or down-hearted at first, but then had a change of attitude and all of a sudden rose above it, found great new meaning in life, and almost always started a national foundation to help others struggling with the same problem.

Is that what I'm supposed to be doing with this? Am I failing, am I sinning, if I don't? I don't have the energy to start a foundation. I'm working on getting from day to day, and I'm not even doing a very good job with that. People don't want to hear that, but it's the truth.

What I'm asking right now is would you come to my house today? Would you just sit with me and be beside me and keep me company through this day? Would you lay your hand on my forehead like you're checking for fever? Would you put your arm around my shoulders when I droop under the load? Can I lean against you without words and sigh and be comforted?

Right now I don't feel like reaching out to anyone; I just feel as if life is a lot of very hard work. If that's sin, please forgive it. If that's frailty, please accept it. Whatever I need, please grant it.

—Karen Batdorf

May God our healer continue the journey of hope begun in you, allowing you to know seasons of joy and peace, relationships of warmth and faithfulness. Amen

—Kathleen Fischer and Thomas Hart

We who lived in concentration camps can remember the men who walked through the huts comforting others, giving away their last piece of bread. They may have been few in number, but they offer sufficient proof that everything can be taken away from a man but one thing: the last of the human freedoms—to choose one's attitude in any given set of circumstances, to choose one's own way.

—Viktor Frankl

God, today I choose to face the one who injured me.
As I look into those eyes that showed no mercy to me,
give me strength to speak the truth.
As I stand up to the one who towered over me
and called forth all my fears,
give me courage to stand firm.
And let my actions be chosen by me:
to be who I am and not what this one who hurt me
would have me to be;
to believe my truth and not the words of the one
who lied to me for so long.
As I wonder where today might lead, lead me on. Amen

—Catherine J. Foote

If one of the prayers that follow appeals to you, take it into your heart and ponder its meaning for your life. Give it time to take root and grow.

I'm tired of the pain / and I want to be healed.
I want / to be healed.

O my God / where are you?

I bless and release _____ / to the Holy Spirit.

Clear truth and stern love / lead me.

Others understand. / They will light my path.

Make me not afraid / to love.

I will fear no evil / for thou art with me.

You are close / to the brokenhearted,
those whose spirit is crushed / you will save.

You know / the whole truth.

As for my response to the men who killed my mother . . . I did not feel hatred for them, and sent to them New Testaments with words of God's love underlined. This was not my to my credit, or of my doing. Nor was it a crazy kind of repressed anger. It was simply a gift from God, who spared me the pain of hating. Why I was given this gift I don't know. I neither prayed for it nor sought it in any other way. I did not even consciously receive it. No one should ever feel lesser for not being given this gift of forgiveness nor better for receiving it. The gift was simply there for me. Dear sister, I hold you in the light, Cindy.

—Cindy Moe-Lobeda, from a letter to a friend

Thirteen years ago my daughter was killed. The city had helped us look for her for six-and-a-half weeks and we wanted to thank everyone, so we held a news conference.

During the news conference we were asked, "What would your reaction be to the murderer if he were found?" Both my husband and I come from a Mennonite background, and we grabbed the only word that we thought would help us through. We said that we would forgive, not knowing what that word really meant.

Well, as we tried to forgive, I discovered that it did not spare us from the journey that we had to walk with our hearts. The rage was unreal.

It has been a long, long journey. . . . God is a part of this journey, and we have to allow victims to walk it. God . . . wants to heal us. I had wanted to rush the process. . . . Maybe we have to drop forgiveness and forgetting at the door and just start walking.

—Wilma Derksen, Canada

Adolfo Perez Esquivel, Nobel Peace Prize winner, was imprisoned by the military dictatorship in Argentina and spent eighteen months in solitary confinement. He felt anger, outrage, and depression but ultimately determined he would not seek revenge and try to kill his oppressors if he were set free. Instead, he would work at bringing a new order into being, where life would be sacred and people would live in peace and dignity. In the months after his release from prison, Perez Esquivel was haunted by Jesus' words, "Father, forgive them, for they know not what they do." To Perez Esquivel, the words made no sense, for his torturers had known exactly what they were doing, but suddenly it dawned on him: what his torturers did not know, what they were entirely ignorant of, was that humanity is one, that we are brothers and sisters in the family of God. What his torturers did not know was that Perez Esquivel was not an enemy they were torturing, but a brother. Perez Esquivel concluded that the only way he could communicate that truth to them was to forgive them and to love them.

—Bill Cane

In spite of everything, I still believe that people are really good at heart.

—Anne Frank (1929–1945), Holland

May the God who is our Hope in calamity, our Rescuer in trouble, and our Protection from the assaults of evil bless and keep us through this day and throughout our lives. Amen

—Marchiene Vroon Rienstra

Chapter 7

Being the Church

I ask not only on behalf of these, but also on behalf of those who will believe in me through their word, that they may all be one. As you, Father, are in me and I am in you, may they also be in us, so that the world may believe that you have sent me. The glory that you have given me I have given them, so that they may be one, as we are one, I in them and you in me, that they may become completely one, so that the world may know that you have sent me and have loved them even as you have loved me.

—John 17:20-23

A Christian community either lives by the intercessory prayers of its members for one another, or the community will be destroyed. I can no longer condemn or hate other Christians for whom I pray, no matter how much trouble they cause me. In intercessory prayer the face that may have been strange and intolerable to me is transformed into the face of one for whom Christ died, the face of a pardoned sinner.

—Dietrich Bonhoeffer (1906-1945), Germany

Not long ago I attended a committee meeting of an ecumenical spiritual center. It was a meeting of several hours, discussing the details of scheduling, financial resources, and administrative tasks, just the sort of work I dread. But this was different. Instead of the usual brief, formal opening prayer that we expect at church meetings, this group opened with five or ten minutes of silent prayer and reflection. Then every half hour, whoever held the clock (a rotated responsibility) would signal the group for five minutes of silent prayer. It was like watching a miracle to see how tension and disagreements would dissolve in that five minutes of silence. The whole discussion would take a different tone, a different slant. Answers to problems almost formed by themselves. Everyone seemed refreshed rather than wilted at the end. I had never realized that a business meeting could be as renewing as a retreat. I went away thinking, This is the way Christ intended for the church to interrelate.

—Flora Slosson Wuellner

Question:

Are love and unity fostered among you? Are you exerting your influence that tale-bearing and detraction shall be avoided, and that individual disagreements among you may be prevented? When differences arise, do you endeavor to settle them speedily and in a spirit of meekness and love?

—William Wistar Comfort

❧

If a fellow believer hurts you, go and tell him—work it out between the two of you. If he listens, you've made a friend.

—paraphrase Matthew 18:15, Eugene H. Peterson, *The Message*

❧

Why is it, Lord, that the very people among whom I seek grace are so quick to condemn? They look at me as if they know me, and in that "knowing," they cast me out. . . . We are the community of faith. We are human. We are sinners. I want to belong. I want to forgive and be forgiven. In your abundant grace and loving kindness, move me to a place of forgiveness and healing—and them as well. Amen

—Roberta French

One of the brethren had been insulted by another and he wanted to take revenge. He came to Abbot Sisois and told him what had taken place, saying: "I am going to get even, Father." But the elder besought him to leave the affair in the hands of God. "No," said the brother, "I will not give up until I have made that fellow pay for what he said." Then the elder stood up and began to pray in these terms: "O God, Thou art no longer necessary to us, and we no longer need Thee to take care of us since, as this brother says, we both can and will avenge ourselves." At this the brother promised to give up his idea of revenge.

—Sayings of the Desert Fathers

ℒ❧

Lord, you never promised us a rose garden, but right now we could use a few daisies or zinnias. We feel confused, unsure of where we are, angry because a wrong has been done, and we are unsure who to blame. It ought to be somebody's fault, but even the one who is to blame is so pathetic it hardly seems worth the effort. So we are left with ourselves. Work on us to make us a community of truthfulness, a community where friendships flourish, a community of joy in the good work you have given us. Help us to know how to go on, confident that you have made us characters in the best story since creation, since it is the story of creation. It is good to be your people. Amen

—Stanley Hauerwas

Holy Loving God,

You, better than any, know the troubles we've had. I never thought I'd see the Berlin Wall fall in my lifetime, but it did. And I never thought I'd see the Anderson clan pass the peace with the Olsons, but right here in front of my eyes, I saw it happen this very morning.

How did you do that? Everybody in the town knows about the sexual molestation charges. Some of them were blaming you for letting it happen, when I knew all the time you had nothing to do with it.

In August, when the temperatures got up to 100, we came into church and shivered. We stood like snow statues, frigid and stiff, keeping our distances. It was like death passing through the pews. Your Holy Spirit went away and so did lots of our members. Oh, that hurt.

It got so bad we couldn't take it anymore. Remember the Sunday, when instead of listening to the organ play the hymns, we all started to sing them? Loud! Somebody had the courage to give the Anderson family a hug instead of a cold stare and then crossed over and did the same to the Olsons. The ice broke. We melted in your grace. We put judgement and labels aside and comforted all the ones who were anguished and sorrowful. Instead of whispering about them, we talked to them out loud and prayed for truth and love.

Forgiveness has opened a future in this place. You, God of mercy and abundance, hear my gratitude. Please don't ever take your Holy Spirit away again. Amen

—June Eastvold

O God,
where are you?

Here.
Where?

Here, in this person
and this person and this person.

But Lord,
I loathe some of these people.

I know,
but this is where
you'll find me.

—Ken Walsh

If I cannot find the face of Jesus in the face of those who are my enemies, if I cannot find him in the unbeautiful, if I cannot find him in those who have the "wrong ideas," if I cannot find him in the poor and the defeated, how will I find him in bread and wine, or in the life after death? If I do not reach out in this world to those with whom he has identified himself, why do I imagine that I will want to be with him, and them, in heaven? Why would I want to be for all eternity in the company of those I avoided every day of my life?

—Jim Forest

✍

God is the creator of all human beings, with their differences, their colours, their races, their religions. Be attentive: Every time you draw nearer to your neighbor, you draw nearer to God. Be attentive: Every time you go further from your neighbor, you go further from God.

—sign in the library in Ibillin, an ancient Palestinian village

✍

Show us, good Lord,
the peace we should seek,
the peace we must give,
the peace we can keep,
the peace we must forgo,
and the peace you have given
in Jesus Christ our Lord.

—Caryl Micklem, England

*B*reath Prayers for the church can be prayed in worship, in church groups and meetings, or any time we remember the needs of the church. Sitting in silence with a group and inwardly praying the same prayer for a few minutes connects us with the spirit and with each other.

Make of us a community / O God.
Bring us closer to you / and to each other.

May we be a church / where love can be found.

Peace with you / is not quiet.

Help us practice / what we believe.

We are members / of one body.

We belong to you / and to one another.

God is our peace / God has made us one.

There is one Spirit. / There is one body.
One Spirit. / One body.

May we be one / as God is one.

You asked for my hands
that you might use them for your purpose.
I gave them for a moment, then withdrew them
for the work was hard.

You asked for my mouth
to speak out against injustice.
I gave you a whisper that I might not be accused.

You asked for my eyes
to see the pain of poverty.
I closed them for I did not want to see.

You asked for my life
that you might work through me.
I gave a small part that I might not get too involved.

Lord, forgive my calculated efforts to serve you
only when it is convenient for me to do so,
only in those places where it is safe to do so,
and only with those who make it easy to do so.

Lord, forgive me,
renew me,
send me out
as a usable instrument
that I might take seriously
the meaning of your cross.

　　　　—Jo Seremane, South Africa

Holy Loving God,

There are the folks you send over for peanut butter and jelly sandwiches, hot soup, coffee, and the bags of bagels the shop down the street donates every week. You know them. The Indian guy who is always drunk and pees on the fence. Paul, the mental case who carries the Bible and quotes chapter and verse. The girl in the dirty sweatshirt with IOWA written large across her bosom. The fellow with the eye infections and the big belly who hangs around until closing and then claims whatever sandwiches are left in the box, saying they will do him for the whole week.

The crew from the congregation stands on the corner downtown and hands out the food, some clothes, toothpaste and stuff, and paperback books. The word is the merchants don't like us to be there. Developers have new condos for sale and homeless drifters aren't the kind of neighbors potential buyers want on their porches. They are putting pressure on city council to order us off the streets.

I ask you God, "Where do we go? Where do the folks you send us go? How can we be real people, not just the poor and the rich?"

Forgive us and teach us how to forgive each other. Make us builders of the City of God. Bring us to the crystal fountains where all are healed and filled, where all bathe in your glistening mercy. Amen

—June Eastvold

Bless those who are the church in quiet and unnoticed ways, especially . . .

—World Council of Churches

✍❦

God who has invited us, we want to invite people into our church community, but sometimes we don't know how. We're unsure, overbusy, and some of us are just shy. It's a comfort to cluster around the coffee pot on Sunday morning, and talk with familiar friends. We need that. But we do feel a call to share what we have here. Help us to encourage those in our church who have the gift of friendship and hospitality. Lead us to the people we need, and the people who need us.

—Linda Schumacher

Dear Lord, we pray for those we have left behind in our thinking, those who would be horrified by what has been said amongst us, who would consider us traitors.
We pray for those who are ahead of us, who would consider our little battles as irrelevant for their struggle, whose patience with our hesitations has run out.
We pray for our land, which is your land;
we pray for ourselves, wanting to be your servants.
Show us the way you want us to go,
the role you wish us to play in your redemptive work,
and the courage to place that above all else. Amen

—Klaus Nurnberger, "Prayer at the end of a conference"

May God kindle in us the fire of love, to bring us alive and give warmth to the world.

—author unknown

Chapter 8

Living As One Nation

O God, we have been recipients of the choicest blessings of heaven. We have been preserved, these many years, in peace and prosperity. We have grown in numbers, wealth, and power as no other nation has ever grown; but we have forgotten God. We have forgotten the gracious hand which preserved us in peace, and multiplied and enriched and strengthened us; and we have vainly imagined, in the deceitfulness of our hearts, that all these blessings were produced by some superior wisdom and virtue of our own. Intoxicated with unbroken success, we have become too self-sufficient to feel the necessity of redeeming and preserving grace, too proud to pray to the God that made us.

It behooves us, then, to humble ourselves . . . to confess our national sins, and to pray for clemency and forgiveness.

—Abraham Lincoln (1809-1865)

Bless our beautiful land, O Lord,
with its wonderful variety of people,
of races, cultures and languages.
May we be a nation
of laughter and joy,
of justice and reconciliation,
of peace and unity,
of compassion, caring and sharing.
We pray this prayer for a true patriotism,
in the powerful name of Jesus our Lord.

—Desmond Mpilo Tutu, South Africa

Our father, who art in Heaven, hallowed be thy name. Thy
Kingdom come. Thy will be done, on earth as it is in Heaven. Give
us this day our daily bread. And forgive us our trespasses, as we
have forgiven those who trespass against us. For if we haven't, there
isn't much point in going any further. But if we have, then we dare
ask for two great favours: to be delivered from all evil and to learn
to live together in peace. For thine is the Kingdom, the Power and
the Glory for ever and ever. Amen

—Pax Christi, United Kingdom

Prayer—living in the presence of God—is the most radical peace action we can imagine. Prayer is peacemaking and not simply the preparation before, the support during, and the thanksgiving after.

—Henri J.M. Nouwen (1932-1996)

❧

Eternal God, help us to look for justice.
Remind us that we are a people dedicated to freedom
and that our true freedom is to do your will.

Guide those who carry the heavy burden of responsibility.
While others are swearing at them,
teach us to pray for them.

We live in a land where the people decide what is going to be.
Help us, the people of this land,
to pray for the right,
to search for the right,
to find the right,
to do the right.

We pray for the sake of Jesus Christ. Amen

—Andrew W. Blackwood, Jr.

Former Soviet leader Nikita Khrushchev was once giving a speech, when suddenly an angry voice in the audience demanded, "Where were you when Stalin was committing his atrocities?" The room fell into stunned silence. Khrushchev's gaze slowly scanned the audience. He asked, "Who said that? Stand up. Identify yourself." Fear gripped every heart. No one moved. No one answered. "My friend," said Khrushchev finally, "where you are right now [that is, too frightened to come forward] is just where I was when Stalin was in power."

—Diane Berke

We regard our living together not as an unfortunate mishap warranting endless competition among us, but as a deliberate act of God to make us a community of brothers and sisters, jointly involved in the quest for a composite answer to the varied problems of life.

—Steven Biku, South African civil rights leader who died in jail in 1977

An old rabbi once asked his pupils how they could tell when the night had ended and the day had begun.

"Could it be," asked one student, "when you can see an animal in the distance and tell whether it's a sheep or a dog?"

"No," answered the rabbi.

Another asked, "Is it when you can look at a tree in the distance and tell whether it's a fig tree or a peach tree?"

"No," answered the rabbi.

"Then what is it?" the pupils demanded.

"It is when you can look on the face of any woman or man and see that it is your sister or brother. Because if you cannot see this, it is still night."

—Martin Buber

❧

God, forgive us.
God, deliver us.
For we have accepted the gifts of many
while rejecting their body-selves
because of color, ethnicity, gender, age,
disability, sexual orientation, appearance.

Help us to celebrate another's value
by the fruits,
not the shape of the tree.

—Chris Glaser

"*I*" and "you," "us" and "them," "winning" and "losing," "victor" and "vanquished"—these are no more than the tricks of the mind exiled from the heart. The face we see before us is no other than our own, the person we see before us is ourselves in another guise. What else can we do but open our hearts, what else do we need to do?

—Christina Feldman

ℒ♥

God help me to weave a tapestry of love and not hate in my children, a spirit of tolerance and caring, and a dedication to freedom for all and not just some. God help me to sow seeds of peace and justice in my children's hearts today.

—Marian Wright Edelman

ℒ♥

Almighty God, whose son came to earth to dwell with the lowly and simple, with the victims of violence and crisis, and with the outcasts and rejected of society; may we keep the same company.

—Prayer from Pakistan

Let my heart be broken with the things that break the heart of God.

—Dr. Robert Pierce

⁂

Lord, when did we see you hungry?
I was hungry and you were flying around the moon.
I was hungry and you told me to wait.
I was hungry and you formed a committee.
I was hungry and you talked about other things.
I was hungry and you told me: "There is no reason."
I was hungry and you had bills to pay for weapons.
I was hungry and you told me: "Now machines do that kind of work."
I was hungry and you said: "Law and order come first."
I was hungry and you said: "There are always poor people."
I was hungry and you said: "My ancestors were hungry too."
I was hungry and you said: "After age fifty, no one will hire you."
I was hungry and you said: "God helps those in need."
I was hungry and you said: "Sorry, stop by again tomorrow."

—anonymous, twentieth-century Lutheran prayer, France

*M*y country, my dear homeland, is sick when she's a bastion for the rich and no refuge for the poor; when fulfillment is a luxury for the few and hope dies of starvation. In heartless success is failure.

—Gerhard E. Frost

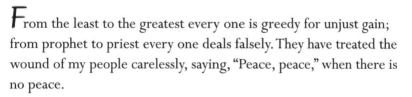

*A*n offender can be punished . . . But to punish and not to restore, that is the greatest of all offenses . . . If we take unto ourselves God's right to punish, then we must also take upon ourselves God's promise to restore.

—Alan Paton (1903-1988), South Africa

*F*rom the least to the greatest every one is greedy for unjust gain; from prophet to priest every one deals falsely. They have treated the wound of my people carelessly, saying, "Peace, peace," when there is no peace.

—Jeremiah 8:10-11

Abraham Heschel never lost the capacity for outrage. During the war years he spoke to a Stanford University ethics class. It turned out that a friend of one of the students, both of whom were Jewish, was producing napalm. The student asked Heschel what she should say to him. "Go to him," Heschel replied, with barely concealed trembling of limb, "and tell him that if he continues making napalm he forfeits the name of Jew. Go to him and tell him . . . that if he continues to be part of such inhuman destructiveness he sins against creation and the Creator. Go to him and plead with him to repent and ask for mercy while there is still time to do so."

—John C. Merkle

Dear God, what the world calls news is almost always
stories of violence, pollution, oppression.
It terrifies me.
It weighs me down.
It sits on my stomach.
The world overwhelms me.

With all the strength of my tired arms
I now drag it all to you.
With a final sigh
I heave it onto your altar.
I cannot fix it.
I offer it all to you.

Now that my arms are empty,
do not let them be idle.
Today let me scatter seeds and bread at the base of a tree
to give something to your beleaguered creation.
Let me reach into my pocket to search for a gift.
Do not let me decide that the gift is too small.
Let me be ready to reach out to the person with hidden needs
who will cross my path today.
Let me help you just the littlest bit.
give me small good things to do today.

 —Karen Batdorf

Lord, teach me the meaning of Your commandment to love our enemies, and help me to obey it. Make me the instrument of Your love, which is not denied to the hungry, the sick, the prisoner, the enemy.

Teach me to hate division, and not to seek after it. But teach me also to stand up for those things that I believe to be right, no matter what the consequences may be.

And help me this day to do some work of peace for You, perhaps to one whom I had thought to be my enemy.

—Alan Paton, South Africa (1903-1988)

Do not depend on the hope of results. When you are doing . . . an apostolic work [such as work for peace], you may have to face the fact that your work will be apparently worthless and even achieve no result at all, if not perhaps results opposite to what you expect. As you get used to the idea, you start more and more to concentrate not on the results but on the value, the rightness, the truth of the work itself. And there too a great deal has to be gone through, as gradually you struggle less for an idea and more and more for specific people. The range tends to narrow down, but it gets much more real. In the end, it is the reality of personal relationships that saves everything.

—Thomas Merton (1915-1968)

I never look at the masses as my responsibility. I look only at the individual. I can love only one person at a time. I can feed only one person at a time.

Just one, one, one.

You get closer to Christ by coming closer to each other. As Jesus said, "Whatever you do to the least of my brethren, you do it to me."

So you begin . . . I begin.

I picked up one person—maybe if I didn't pick up that one person I wouldn't have picked up all the others.

The whole work is only a drop in the ocean. But if we don't put the drop in, the ocean would be one drop less.

Same thing for you. Same thing in your family. Same thing in the church where you go. Just begin . . . one, one, one.

—Mother Teresa (1910-1997), India

*W*e cannot love issues, but we can love people, and the love of people reveals to us the way to deal with issues.

— Henri J.M. Nouwen (1932-1996)

*A*t some thoughts one stands perplexed—especially at the sight of sin—and wonders whether one should use force or humble love. Always decide to use humble love. If you resolve on that, once and for all, you may subdue the whole world. Loving humility is marvelously strong, the strongest of all things, and there is nothing else like it.

— Fyodor Dostoyevsky (1820-1881), Russia

*T*oday's problem is not atomic energy but man's heart. Peace cannot be kept by force. It can only be achieved by understanding.

— Albert Einstein

Breath Prayers for our country will be as unique as the people who pray them. Pray when you remember the needs that you are most concerned about, the people that are trying to help, and especially whenever you think of the situations that look most hopeless.

Through our lives / and by our prayers
your kingdom / come.

Open my mind / my eyes, my heart.

Love us / into action.

May anger and fear / give way to love.

May the powerless / find power.

O savior of the poor / liberate your people.

May people think / to befriend one another.

Father, forgive us. / We do not know what we are doing.

In my own lifetime I have seen incredible changes in the world. Yes, we do have terrible problems and perplexities. Yes, evil is very much alive and reaches us in new, insidious ways. As from the beginning of recorded history, there are still wars, devastations, destructions. But I do not believe that we are to wait, expecting the worst, counting on a wrathful God to end everything in a single ruinous blow. Jesus told us he is with us forever, among us now, working with us, his vast kingdom of transforming love spreading quietly but ever more deeply.

We can see changes wrought by Jesus' love if we do not allow ourselves to be terrorized by predictors of doom. There was no United Nations when I was a child; war was still glorified; lynchings were still common; domestic abuse was denied and covered up; there was little equality or justice for women in politics, ministry, business, academia, medicine; there were few interracial schools. . . . There was little if any concern over pollution of air, earth, and water. The lakes and rivers were almost dead with toxic wastes. If anyone fought for whales, seals, or redwood trees, I never heard of them. There was no welfare program.

At that same time, nations and churches did not ask one another's forgiveness, ever. There was little awareness or compassion for political and natural disasters in other lands. There was no feeling of this being one world.

There is a change in spite of our many problems. We are beginning to listen to one another. We are admitting need for changes. In an almost unbelievable way concern and compassion for the suffering have deepened. Christ is at work among us, just as he promised. The meek are beginning to be heard. In my lifetime there has been a Gandhi, a Martin Luther King, Jr., a Mother Teresa, a Nelson Mandela, and each has been heard and honored around the world.

—Flora Slosson Wuellner

May the God of justice and mercy unite us in compassionate solidarity with all those in need, that our lives may be just and merciful, and a source of blessing to many. Amen

—Marchiene Vroon Rienstra

Chapter 9

And on Earth, Peace

*W*e struggled against one another: now we are reconciled to struggle for one another.

We believed it was right to withstand one another: now we are reconciled to understand one another.

We endured the power of violence: now we are reconciled to the power of tolerance.

We built irreconcilable barriers between us: now we seek to build a society of reconciliation.

We suffered a separateness that did not work: now we are reconciled to make togetherness work.

We believed we alone held the truth: now we are reconciled in the knowledge that truth holds us.

—South African national service of thanksgiving

O God, we thank You for this worship time. We pray that all ways of all peoples come together in understanding. We pray that world leaderships come together to end the needless waste of war spending. We pray that the ways of the Native people live on. We pray that our environment becomes cleaner and less polluted. We pray for our friends who are sick and need help. O God, we pray for this world so that all these nuclear weapons and other bad things that we point at each other will some day soon be all destroyed. We pray that adversaries will communicate and all of the mistrust will be healed. We pray for the renewal of our Mother Earth. We thank You again for this ceremony. *Hetchetu aloh.* (It is good.) *Mitaquye oyasin.* (All is related. All the four-legged, the winged, the swimming, the two-legged, even the rock, are related to one another and all are equal.)

—Eagle Man, Lakota

✿

I am weary of the dark voices crying out doom;
I am weary of the fearful voices crying out only for their nation;
I am weary of the disinherited voices crying out in hopelessness;
let my voice sing the laughter of God;
let my voice sing good news to the poor;
let my voice sing restitution of the oppressed;
let my voice sing healing of the violated;
let my voice sing the return of the banned;
let my voice be the laughter of God. Amen

—Robin Green, USPG, England

*I*f you, even you, had only recognized on this day the things that make for peace!

    —Luke 19:42

✒

*C*ome let us go up to the mountain of the Lord, that we may walk the paths of the Most High. And we shall beat our swords into plowshares, and our spears into pruning hooks. Nation shall not lift up sword against nation—neither shall they learn war anymore. And none shall be afraid, for the mouth of the Lord of Hosts has spoken.

    —Jewish prayer for peace

✒

*B*lessed are the peacemakers, for they shall be known as the Children of God. But I say to you that hear, love your enemies, do good to those who hate you, bless those who curse you, pray for those who abuse you. To those who strike you on the cheek, offer the other also, and from those who take away your cloak, do not withhold your coat as well. Give to everyone who begs from you and of those who take away your goods, do not ask them again. And as you wish that others would do to you, do so to them.

    —Christian prayer for peace

In a time such as this, when we have been seriously and most cruelly hurt by those who hate us, and when we must consider ourselves to be gravely threatened by those same people, it is hard to speak of the ways of peace and to remember that Christ enjoined us to love our enemies, but this is no less necessary for being difficult.

—Wendell Berry

Pray before all else, otherwise whatever we attempt will fail. Pray for the victims, their families, their caregivers, ourselves. Can we pray for the perpetrators too? We must! Otherwise the fear and the anger we feel will overwhelm us. If we can not bring ourselves to forgive at this moment, let us at least pray for the grace to want to forgive and to want to pray for our enemies. Father, forgive us, as we forgive those who trespass against us. Pray, too, that no more blood be shed to pay for this crime.

—Tom Cornell

To confront evil successfully, we as a nation must also confront our own darkness; we must act not as a messiah, filled with undue majesty and certainty, but rather as a healer, filled with compassion, empathy, and humility.

—David Spangler

I ask my Lord in the manger, while kneeling before Him, in full repentance: Lord, make the good life of justice, security, and reconciliation possible for all of us here in the land where you became human. Lord of peace and good will, put an end to bloodshed, violence, and war. Allow all our children, Israeli and Palestinian, to experience just peace, a secure future, and the power of forgiveness and love.

—Munib A. Younan, Lutheran Bishop in Jerusalem

A special prayer was added by the Serbian Church to the Holy Liturgy early in the breakdown of Yugoslavia. It includes this petition: "For all those who commit injustice against their neighbors, whether by causing sorrow to orphans, spilling innocent blood or by returning hatred for hatred, that God will grant them repentance, enlighten their minds and their hearts and illumine their souls with the light of love even toward their enemies, let us pray to the Lord."

—Jim Forest

O God of earth and altar,
bow down and hear our cry;
our earthly rulers falter,
our people drift and die;
the walls of gold entomb us,
the swords of scorn divide,
take not thy thunder from us,
but take away our pride.

From all that terror teaches,
from lies of tongue and pen,
from all the easy speeches,
that comfort cruel men,
from sale and profanation
of honour and the sword,
from sleep and from damnation,
deliver us, good Lord!

—G.K. Chesterton (1874-1936), England

Where there is gunfire, let there be silence.
Where there is silence, let there be laughter.
Where there is laughter, let there be light.
Where there is light, let there be love.
Where there is love, let there be hope.
Where there is hope, let there be you.
Where there is you, let there be life.

—Leonardo Alishan, "Little Prayer"

O God, to those who have hunger give bread;
and to those who have bread give the hunger for justice.

—Latin American prayer

Throughout the Bible God appears as the liberator of the oppressed. He is not neutral. He does not attempt to reconcile Moses and Pharaoh, to reconcile the Hebrew slaves with their Egyptian oppressors or to reconcile the Jewish people with any of their later oppressors. Oppression is sin and it cannot be compromised with, it must be done away with. God takes sides with the oppressed. As we read in Psalm 103:6, "God, who does what is right, is always on the side of the oppressed."

—from the Kairos Document, South Africa

We join with the earth and with each other
to bring new life to the land,
to restore the waters,
to refresh the air.

We join with the earth and with each other
to renew the forests,
to care for the plants,
to protect the creatures.

We join with the earth and with each other
to celebrate the seas,
to rejoice in the sunlight,
to sing the song of the stars.

We join with the earth and with each other
to recreate the human community,
to promote justice and peace,
to remember our children.

We join with the earth and with each other.
We join together as many and diverse expressions
of one loving mystery: for the healing of the
earth and the renewal of all life.

—Pat Mathes Cane, U.N. Environmental Sabbath Program

Life darkens.
I ask peace.

Peace to people
who live outside
the American Dream.
Peace to people
who work hard
like some in my country,
every day carrying burdens,
but laying down anger,
bearing the good weight
of feeding family,
the true weight
of an honest living,
the endless weight of the world,
the beautiful weight
of carrying without violence.

Peace to people in my country.
Peace to people who watch the news
but do not believe
all they hear and see,
and do not revere revenge.

Peace to people of faith.
Peace to people who have been scarred
yet choose another way.

Peace to men and women
who refuse to hate,
who show their children
love.

May those who suffer the selfish
not blame the unknowing,
who would wish them will.
May they wish ill upon no one.

May we all hold hope
despite leaders who see
no other way but war.
In the depths of night
may we recall our source
beyond devilment
and bitterness
in every land.

May searching folk the world around
find peace
within themselves.
May this peace grow.

     —Gregor Stark, "An American Peace Prayer"

*W*e as "Peace People" believe in taking down the barriers, but we also believe in the most energetic reconciliation among peoples by getting them to know each other, talk each other's languages, understand each others fears and beliefs . . . . The only force which can break down barriers is the force of love, the force of truth, soul force. . . .

To those who say that we are naïve, utopian idealists, we say that we are the only realists, and that those who continue to support militarism in our time are supporting the progress towards total self-destruction of the human race.

—Betty Williams

*W*alk together, talk together, O you people of the earth, and then, only then, can you have peace.

—The Vedas, compiled c. 1080-500 B. C. E., oldest Hindu Sanskrit texts

*I*n a world of flawed communication, community is possible
through understanding others.
In a world of painful alienation, community is created
by accepting others.
In a world of broken trust, community is sustained by forgiveness.

—David Augsburger

*J*ohn of the Cross knew all about God's love: "Where there is no
love," he said, "sow love—and you will reap love." I like better the
modification by a pragmatic Dominican working in the Peace
Camps in Israel. "Where there is no love," he says, "sow love, and
somebody will reap love."

That makes more sense to me. We must have the blind faith to
be compassionate and to forgive, but we must know quite clearly
that we ourselves may not live to see the tree we have planted
bear fruit.

But compassion and non-violence do bear fruit: of that I am
certain. Perhaps it would be more accurate to say that compassion
and non-violent resistance to aggression are fruit: fruits of the
spirit, free gifts of God. I believe too that forgiveness is not so
much a virtue we are called to practice but a gift for which we
must pray.

—Sheila Cassidy, England

*H*aving no gift of strategy or arms,
no secret weapon and no walled defense,
I shall become a citizen of love,
that little nation with the blood-stained sod
where even the slain have power, the only country
that sends forth an ambassador to God.

Renouncing self and crying out to evil
to end its wars, I seek a land that lies
all unprotected like a sleeping child;
nor is my journey reckless and unwise.
Who doubts that love has an effective weapon
may meet with a surprise.

  —Jessica Powers (1905-1988), "The Little Nation"

Pray not for Arab or Jew, for Palestinian or Israeli,
but pray rather for yourselves
that you may not divide them in your prayers,
but keep them both together in your hearts.

—Elias Chacour, Palestinian Christian

Since our inner world is reflected in our outer world, peace, joy,
and love (the fruits of forgiveness) will flow into the world's
environment and help people who are having difficulty forgiving
themselves or others. The more people who forgive, the stronger
the influence in the world for the forgiveness of injuries large and
small, even the deep-rooted, age-old hatreds between people of
different nationalities and religions.

—Theresa Magness

O God, help us not to despise or oppose what we do not
understand.

—William Penn (1644-1718)

Breath prayer is my best weapon against denial and withdrawal.
I use it when I read the paper or listen to the news; sometimes when
the news is bad, I use it all day.

—Pamela Grenfell Smith

And on earth / peace.

Peace / to all children.

The peace for which we pray / is possible.

Show us how and where / to make a start.

Give us strength to understand / and eyes to see.

May we see / the truth.

We are many / we are one.

Strengthen the hands / that work for peace.

Fill your world / with justice and joy.

May all end / in good and blessing.

I am the child who lives on the streets;
Pray for me.
I am the child in a refugee camp;
Pray for me.
I am the child hidden away in an orphanage;
Pray for me.
I am the child trying to find my parents;
Pray for me.
I am the child dying of hunger;
Pray for me.
Share your music, your education, your riches with me.
Share your shoes, your food, your blankets, your fuel, your toys with me.
Share your ideas, your imagination, your skills, your time, your dreams with me.
Share your world with me.
It should be mine as well.

—Children's Aid Direct, London, England

In almost every social studies class I hear the question, "Why do you teach us about hunger, nuclear war, injustice, poverty, and environmental threats, when there is nothing that we can do about them?" In other words don't dump this load on me—it crushes my spirit, deadens my hope, and makes me feel helpless.

Teaching that there are solutions, that there are things I can do to make the world better, and that we can have a hand in shaping our destiny, has a real impact on young people. I see it brighten students' eyes, lighten their spirits, and provide hope.

—Jim Jarvis, high school teacher, Chicago

May God bless you with the discomfort at easy answers, half-truths, and superficial relationships, so that you will live deep in your heart.

May God bless you with anger at injustice, oppression, and exploitation of people and the earth so that you will work for justice, equity, and peace.

May God bless you with tears to shed for those who suffer so you will reach out your hands to comfort them and change their pain into joy.

And may God bless you with the foolishness to think that you can make a difference in the world, so you will do the things which others say cannot be done.

—Franciscan Prayer

We are amputees.
Before, we were soldiers,
members of different armies
that laid landmines
and blew the legs
and arms and eyes
off one another.
Now we teach and learn together
in The Centre of the Dove.
We beg the world to stop making mines.
We beg the world to stop laying mines.
We beg for funds for clearing mines
so that we can rebuild our families,
our village and our country again.

　　—Hem Phang, Kleang Vann, Channa Reth, Chreuk, four former
soldiers of opposing factions in Cambodia's long civil war who make
wheelchairs together at the Centre of the Dove. Together, they wrote
an open letter asking others to join their petition for a ban on landmines. To date, more than 1.5 million signatures are on record
around the world. Translated by Mr. Seak Meng.

Although the world is full of suffering, it is also full of the
overcoming of it.

　　—Helen Keller

I give thanks to God
because he has not left me alone in the world,
that I have a family that I love very much
and that they love me also.
I would like it if everyone in the world
had a family and that being together
could feel the warmth of love and care
the same as I feel.
Almighty God, I would like that there would be
no more hungry children in the world,
that people would stop thinking of killing
and would help the people that are so poor. Amen

    —a child's prayer, Puerto Rico

*M*ay the God who cares passionately for the earth and all that
lives in it bless us with the same caring compassion and preserve us
from greed and violence, now and always. Amen

    —Marchiene Vroon Rienstra

The year was the decade-maker, 1970—
Along a German street, head down, stomach empty,
walked a young man totally alone.
"Who are you, young man?"
"I am Mudeer, I fled Pakistan to escape—
I was turned back from England where my sister lives.
I cannot speak German and I am afraid."
"Come home with me. You need have no fear.
Let us first get you something to eat."
Unto us a son was given!
Later two grandchildren call us, "God Parents."
Mudeer is a Muslim, and I am a Christian,
and in the universe somewhere
God is smiling.

     —Richard Wilcox, Spain, "Unto Us a Son Was Given"

Blessed be.

    —Ancient Celtic blessing

Acknowledgments

Page 8: 1 John 4:7 (NRSV)

Page 8: Joel 2:13 (NRSV)

Page 8: "Lord, let me return to you," Preparatory Service for the Days of Awe by Chaim Stern, in *Gates of Forgiveness,* edited by Chaim Stern. (New York: Central Conference of American Rabbis, 1993). Used by permission.

Page 9: "Spirit of comfort and longing," Janet Morley in *Celebrating Women* edited by Hannah Ward, Jennifer Wild, and Janet Morley. (London: SPCK, 1995).

Page 9: "God help us to find our confession," from *The Prayer Tree* by Michael Leunig. (Prymble, Australia: HarperCollins Publishers, 1973). Used by permission of HarperCollins Publishers.

Page 10: "O God of grace," The Reverend Jean Dalby Clift in *Women's Uncommon Prayers,* edited by Elizabeth Rankin Geitz, Marjorie A. Burke, and Ann Smith. (Harrisburg, Pa.: Morehouse Publishing, 2000). Used by permission of The Reverend Jean Dalby Clift.

Page 10: "I have knowingly and willingly disobeyed you, Lord" from *Creative Brooding* by Robert A. Raines. (New York: The Macmillan Company, 1966).

Page 11: "Repentence has nothing to do with self-torment," from *Seventy Times Seven: The Power of Forgiveness* by Johann Christoph Arnold. (Farmington, Pa.: Plough Publishing House, 1997). Used by permission. ✍♥

Page 11: "We must not despair," letter from a Russian monk in *A Monastery Kitchen,* revised edition by Brother Victor Antoine d'Avila Latourrette. (New York: Harper & Row Publishers, Inc., 1989).

Page 12: "We come before you today, Lord," by Holly Jo Turnquist Fischer, Northfield, Minnesota. Used by permission.

Page 13: "Merciful Healer, enter those deep, dark places," from *Forgiveness, The Passionate Journey* by Flora Slosson Wuellner. (Nashville: Upper Room Books, 2001). Copyright © 2001 Flora Slosson Wuellner. Used by permission of Upper Room Books. ✍♥

Page 13: "God in heaven, you have helped my life," a Nigerian Christian in *Prayers of African Religion,* edited by John Mbiti. (Maryknoll: Orbis 1976).

Page 14: "Gracious God, humble us through the violence of your love," from *Prayers Plainly Spoken* by Stanley Hauerwas. (Downers Grove, Ill.: InterVarsity Press, 1999). Copyright © 1999 Stanley Hauerwas. Used by permission of InterVarsity Press, PO Box 1400, Downers Grove, IL 60515. www.ivpress.com.

Page 14: "For our age, prayer must be the bringing," Ann and Barry Ulanov, in *The Study of Spirituality* edited by Jones, Wainwright, and Yarnold. (London: SPCK, 1986).

Page 15: "We come to you in penitence, confessing our sins," William Sloane Coffin, Jr, in *Prayers from Riverside,* edited by Leo S. Thorne. (Cleveland: Pilgrim Press, 1983), 21. Copyright © 1983 The Pilgrim Press. Adapted by permission.

Page 16: "Lord Christ, help us to have the courage and humility," Kathy Galloway in *The Complete Book of Christian Prayer,* edited by SPCK. (New York: Continuum, 1997).

Page 18: "I have already confessed my sins to you, God," by Karen Batdorf, Minneapolis, Minnesota. Used by permission.

Page 20: "Nobody has to sit about being humilated," Dorothy L. Sayers in *Unpopular Opinions: Twenty-One Essays* (New York: Harcourt, Brace, 1947).

Page 20: James 5:16 (NRSV)

Page 21: "I'm weary of being sorry," by Lyn Klug, Amery, Wisconsin. Used by permission.

Page 22: "A woman doesn't meet her God every day," from *On the Doorposts of Your House,* edited by Chaim Stern. (New York: Central Conference of American Rabbis, 1993). Used by permission.

Page 22: "The voice of despair says, 'I sin over and over again,'" from *The Road to Daybreak* by Henri J. M. Nouwen. (New York: Doubleday 1988). Copyright © 1988 Henri J. M. Nouwen. Used by permission of Doubleday, a division of Random House, Inc.

Page 23: "No matter how far we have wandered," from *Forgiveness* by Archbishop Daniel E. Pilarczyk. (Huntington, Ind.: Our Sunday Visitor, 1992). Used by permission of Archbishop Daniel E. Pilarczyk.

Page 24: "Peace and love are always in us, being and working," from *Meditations with Julian of Norwich Introductions and Versions* by Brendan Doyle. (Rochester, Vt.: Bear & Company, 1983). Copyright © 1983 Bear & Company, Inc. Used by permission.

Page 25: "If God pleases to forget anything, then He can forget it," George Macdonald (1824-1905), Scotland.

Page 25: "When the thought of God," by Søren Kierkegaard in *The Search for God* by David Manning White. (New York: Macmillan, including Collier Macmillan, Canada, Inc., 1983).

Page 27: "Forgiveness is not just the cancelling of a debt," from *A Private House of Prayer* by Leslie Weatherhead (London: Hodder & Stoughton, Ltd, 1958), p. 137.

Page 27: "Who is closer to God," from *The Heart of God* by Joan D. Chittister, OSB. (Erie, Pa.: Benetvision, 2000). Used by permission of Benetvision. ℒ♥

Page 28: "Savior, for this long road that has wound," from *Prayers for a Time of Crisis* by Walter Riess. (St. Louis, Mo.: Concordia Publishing House, 1966).

Page 28: "Light breaks upon the heart," from *On the Doorposts of Your Heart* by Chaim Stern (New York: Central Conference of American Rabbis, 1993). Used by permission.

Page 29: "Glory to thee, my God this night," Thomas Ken (1637-1711), England.

Page 29: "Heavenly Father, as I count your many blessings," by Catherine Coyle, Madison, Wisconsin. Used by permission.

Page 30: "Lord, let no unnecessary sense of guilt," from *Instrument of Thy Peace* by Alan Paton. (New York: The Seabury Press, 1968). Copyright © 1968, 1982 the Seabury Press, Inc. Reprinted by permission of HarperCollins Publishers, Inc.

Page 31: "Without forgiveness there is no love," from *Living with Contradiction: Reflections on the Rule of St. Benedict* by Esther De Waal. (Grand Rapids, Mich.: Zondervan, 1989). Used by permission of Zondervan.

Page 31: "May the God of gentleness," from *Swallow's Nest: A Feminine Reading of the Psalms* by Marchiene Vroon Rienstra. (Grand Rapids, Mich.: Wm. B. Eerdmans Publishing Company, 1992). Copyright © 1992 Wm. B. Eerdmans Publishing Company, Grand Rapids, Mich. Used by permission.

Page 34: "Lord, make me an instrument of your peace," anonymous, commonly called The Prayer of St. Francis.

Page 36: Ephesians 4:32 (NRSV)

Page 36: Colossians 3:12-14 (NRSV)

Page 36: "When the apostles asked Jesus," M. Basil Pennington in *Reflections on Forgiveness and Spiritual Growth,* edited by Andrew J. Weaver and Monica Furlong. (Nashville: Abingdon Press 2000). Copyright © 2000 Abingdon Press. Used by permission. ✠

Page 37: John 20:23, from *The Message* by Eugene Peterson. (Colorado Springs, Colo.: NavPress 1993). Copyright © Eugene H. Peterson 1993, 1994, 1995. Used by permission of NavPress Publishing Group.

Page 37: "Truth without love kills," by Eberhard Arnold (1883-1935).

Page 37: "Forgiveness does not mean we suppress our anger," from *Illuminata* by Marianne Williamson. (New York: Random House, 1994).

Page 38: "O my Lord—wash me," author unknown in *The Complete Book of Christian Prayer* edited by SPCK. (New York: Continuum, 1997).

Page 38: "Lord, take away this cup of bitterness," Jane Robson. Used by permission of Jane Robson.

Page 39: "Lord, this is what went wrong," from *The Book of a Thousand Prayers*, Zondervan edition by Angela Ashwin. Copyright © 1996, 2002 by Angela Ashwin. Used by permission of Zondervan.

Page 39: "Write the wrongs that are done to you in sand," Arabic Proverb in *Prayers for Healing: 365 Blessings, Poems, and Meditations from around the World,* edited by Maggie Oman. (Berkeley, Calif.: Conari Press, 2000).

Page 40: "Forgiveness, far from being merely another human activity," from *Letter from Taizé 1999 no. 3.* Copyright © Ateliers et Presses de Taizé, 71250 Taizé Community, France. Used by permission.

Page 40: "I really must digress to tell you a bit of good news," from page 106-107 in *Letters to Malcolm: Chiefly on Prayer.* Copyright © 1964, 1963 by C.S. Lewis PTE Ltd. and renewed 1992, 1991 by Arthur Owen Barfield. Reprinted by permission of Harcourt, Inc.

Page 41: "Each time I think I've learned to handle hurt," from *Songs for Silent Moments* by Lois Walfrid Johnson. Copyright © 1980 Lois Walfrid Johnson. Used by permission.

Page 41: "I think that in order to really have a forgiving sense," from *To Forgive is Human* by Michael E. McCullough, Steven J. Sandage, and Everett L. Worthington, Jr. (Downer's Grove, Ill.: InterVarsity Press, 1997). Used by permission of InterVarsity Press, PO Box 1400, Downers Grove, IL 60515. www.ivpress.com.

Page 42: "Dear Lord, help me release my need to control," from *Come Apart for Awhile* by Robert and Janet Ellsworth. (Lee's Summit, Mo.: Pathfinders Ministry 1995). Used by permission of Pathfinders Ministry, PO Box 2302, Lee's Summit, MO 64063-7302, 816-525-7068.

Page 42: "God of tears and God of laughter," from *Praying with Body and Soul* by Jane Vennard. Copyright © 1998 Augsburg Fortress, p. 68.

Page 43: "Give me this night, O God, the peace of mind which is truly rest," author unknown in *The Complete Book of Christian Prayer* edited by SPCK. (New York: Continuum, 1997).

Page 44: "Abbot Pastor said," from *The Wisdom of the Desert,* translated by Thomas Merton. (New York: New Directions Publishing Corporation, 1960). Copyright © 1960 by The Abbey of Gethsemani, Inc. Reprinted by permission of New Directions Publishing Corp. and Pollinger Limited, London, England.

Page 44: "Perhaps the most important thing we bring," ("A Place of Refuge") from *My Grandfather's Blessings* by Rachel Naomi Remen, M.D. (New York: The Berkeley Publishing Group, 2000). Copyright © 2000 by Rachel Naomi Remen, M.D. Used by permission of Riverhead Books, a division of Penguin Putnam, Inc.

Page 45: "In the name of the living Christ," from *Forgiveness, The Passionate Journey* by Flora Slosson Wuellner. (Nashville: Upper Room Books, 2001). Copyright © 2001 Flora Slosson Wuellner. Used by permission of Upper Room Books.

Page 86: "Sometimes I can't find words," from *Still Time to Sing* by Catharine Brandt. Copyright © 1980 Catharine Brandt. Used by permission.

Page 87: "Well, I've burned the beans again," from *It's Me, O Lord* by Anne Springsteen (St. Louis, Mo.: Concordia Publishing House, 1970), p. 48.

Page 88: "However unacceptable the package," from "The Divine Dance in Our Daily Life" by Sheila Morgan in *Fellowship in Prayer,* October 1993. Used by permission of Sheila Morgan.

Page 88: "As I kneel to pray, the sun is setting," from *Liferails* by Scott Walker. Copyright © 1999 Scott Walker, admin. Augsburg Fortress, p. 108.

Page 89: "She's seated in her no-longer-thick-plush green chair," from "I Try to Talk with My Mother-in-Law" by L. Anderson, Marine, Minnesota. Used by permission.

Page 90: "She doesn't know God forgives her," from *Listening to Your Life* by Frederick Buechner. (New York: HarperCollins, 1992). Used by permission of Frederick Buechner. ✍

Page 90: "Let the words of my mouth," by Karen Batdorf, Minneapolis, Minnesota. Used by permission.

Page 92: "O God, this is one of the worst days of my life," by Martin Noll, Amery, Wisconsin. Used by permission.

Page 93: "'Forgive and forget,' they say," by Paul Nieman, Amery, Wisconsin. Used by permission.

Page 94: "Lord, there are two frustrations to my disability," Peter Lockwood in *The Complete Book of Christian Prayer* edited by SPCK. (New York: Continuum, 1997). Used by permission.

Page 96: "Ok, so Lord . . . here's the deal," by Holly Jo Turnquist Fischer, Northfield, Minnesota. Used by permission.

Page 98: "Lord, I bring before you," by Thomas á Kempis from *Prayers from the Imitation of Christ,* edited by Ron Klug. Copyright © 1996 Augsburg Fortress. Used by permission.

Page 99: "In the night I am wide awake," from *Hello Night!* by Herbert Brokering. Copyright © 1999 Augsburg Fortress, p. 67.

Page 102: "Oh, the comfort—the inexpressible comfort," from *A Life for a Life* by Dinah Maria Mulock Craik. Copyright © 1859 Harper & Bros.

Page 102: "Beauty of friendship grow between us," traditional Celtic blessing (c.450–c.700) in *Celtic Blessings: Prayers for Everyday Life* by Ray Simpson. (Chicago: Loyola Press, 1998).

Page 103: "Peace between neighbors, peace between kindred," traditional Celtic blessing (c450-c700).

Page 106: Matthew 5:43-45 (NRSV)

Page 138: "You, better than any, know the troubles we've had," by June Eastvold, Bellingham, Washington. Used by permission.

Page 139: "O God, where are you?" from *Sometimes I Weep: Prayers and Meditations* by Ken Walsh. (Valley Forge: Judson Press, 1973). Copyright © 1973 Judson Press. Used by permission of Judson Press, 800-4-JUDSON. www.judsonpress.com.

Page 140: "If I cannot find the face of Jesus," from *Making Friends of Enemies* by Jim Forest. (New York: Crossroad, 1987). Used by permission of Jim Forest. ℒ♥

Page 140: "Show us, good Lord," from *Contemporary Prayers for Public Worship*, edited by Caryl Micklem. Copyright © 1967 SCM Press. Used by permission.

Page 142: "You asked for my hands," from *Lifelines* by Jo Seremane (Roodepoort, South Africa: Jo Seremane, 1992).

Page 143: "There are folks you send over for peanut butter and jelly sandwiches," by June Eastvold, Bellingham, Washington. Used by permission.

Page 144: "Bless those who are the church," author unknown in *With All God's People: The New Ecumenical Prayer Cycle*. (Geneva, Switzerland: World Council of Churches, 1989).

Page 144: "God who has invited us," by Linda Schumacher, Amery, Wisconsin. Used by permission.

Page 145: "Dear Lord, we pray for those we have left behind," Klaus Nurnberger, reprinted from *Cry Justice: Prayers, Meditations and Readings from South Africa* by John de Gruchy. (Maryknoll, N.Y.: Orbis Books, 1986). Copyright © Klaus Nurnberger. Used by permission.

Page 145: "May God kindle in us the fire of love," author unknown in *The Complete Book of Christian Prayer*, edited by SPCK. (New York: Continuum, 1997).

Page 148: "O God, we have been recipients of the choicest blessings of heaven," Abraham Lincoln (1809-1865).

Page 149: "Bless our beautiful land, O Lord," Desmond Mpilo Tutu, South Africa, from the inauguration of Nelson Mandela as State President of South Africa, 1994, in *2000 Years of Prayer*, compiled by Michael Counsell. (Harrisburg, Pa.: Morehouse Publishing, 1999).

Page 149: "Our father, who art in Heaven, hallowed be thy name," Pax Christi, United Kingdom in *The Way of Peace*, compiled by Hannah Ward and Jennifer Wild. (Oxford, England: Lion, 1999).

Page 150: "Prayer—living in the presence of God," Henri J.M. Nouwen in *Seeds of Hope: A Henri Nouwen Reader*. (New York: Doubleday, 1989, 1997).

Page 150: "Eternal God, help us to look for justice," from *We Need You Here, Lord: Prayers from the City* by Andrew W. Blackwood, Jr. (Grand Rapids, Mich.: Baker Book House 1969). Used by permission of Baker Book House.

Page 151: "Former Soviet leader," from *Love Always Answers: Walking the Path of Miracles* by Diane Berke. (New York: The Crossroad Publishing Company, 1994). Used by permission of Diane Berke.

Page 151: "We regard our living together not as an unfortunate mishap," Steven Biko in *Prayers for Healing: 365 Blessings, Poems, and Meditations from around the World,* edited by Maggie Oman. (Berkeley, CA: Conari Press, 2000).

Page 152: "An old rabbi once asked his pupils," from *Tales of the Hasidim* by Martin Buber. (New York: Schocken Books, 1991).

Page 152: "God forgive us," from *Coming Out to God: Prayers for Lesbians and Gay Men, Their Families and Friends* by Chris Glaser. (Louisville: Westminster John Knox Press, 1991). Copyright © 1991 Chris Glaser. Used by permission of Westminster John Knox Press.

Page 153: "'I' and 'you,' 'us' and 'them,' 'winning' and 'losing,' 'victor' and 'vanquished,'" Christina Feldman in *Peace Prayers: Meditations, Affirmations, Invocations, Poems, and Prayers for Peace,* edited by the staff of HarperSanFrancisco. (New York: HarperCollins Publishers, 1992).

Page 153: "God help me to weave a tapestry of love," from *Guide My Feet* by Marian Wright Edelman. Copyright © 1995 by Marian Wright Edelman. Reprinted by permission of Beacon Press, Boston.

Page 153: "Almighty God, whose son came to earth," Prayer from Pakistan in *A Procession of Prayers: Prayers and Meditations from around the World,* edited by John Carden. (London, England: Cassell and Geneva, Switzerland: World Council of Churches).

Page 154: "Let my heart be broken," Dr. Robert Pierce, founder of Samaritan's Purse.

Page 154: "Lord, when did we see you hungry?" anonymous, twentieth-century Lutheran prayer, France, translated by Mary-Theresa McCarthy in *Prayers for All People,* edited by Mary Ford-Grabowsky. (New York: Doubleday, 1995).

Page 155: "My country, my dear homeland, is sick," from *Seasons of a Lifetime* by Gerhard E. Frost. Copyright © 1989 Augsburg Fortress, p. 141.

Page 155: "An offender can be punished," from *Too Late the Phalarope* by Alan Paton. Reprinted with the permission of Scribner, an imprint of Simon & Schuster Adult Publishing Group. Copyright © 1953 by Alan Paton; copyright renewed © 1981 by Alan Paton.

Page 155: Jeremiah 8:10-11 (NRSV)

Page 156: "Abraham Heschel never lost the capacity for outrage," from *Abraham Joshua Heschel: Exploring His Life and Thought* by John C. Merkle. Macmillan Reference USA., Copyright © 1985, Macmillan Reference, USA. Reprinted by permission of The Gale Group.

Page 157: "Dear God, what the world calls news," by Karen Batdorf, Minneapolis, Minnesota. Used by permission.

Page 158: "Lord, teach me the meaning of Your commandment," from *Instrument of Thy Peace* by Alan Paton. (New York: The Seabury Press, 1968). Copyright © 1968, 1982 The Seabury Press, Inc. Reprinted by permission of HarperCollins Publishers, Inc.

Page 158: "Do not depend on the hope of results," Thomas Merton in *Making Friends of Enemies: Reflections on the Teachings of Jesus* by Jim Forest. (New York: Crossroad, 1987). Used by permission of Jim Forest.

Page 159: "I never look at the masses as my responsibility," from *Works of Love are Works of Peace* by Mother Teresa of Calcutta and the Missionaries of Charity. (San Fransisco: Ignatius Press, 1996).

Page 160: "We cannot love issues," Henri J.M. Nouwen in *Seeds of Hope: A Henri Nouwen Reader.* (New York: Doubleday 1989, 1997).

Page 160: "At some thoughts one stands perplexed," Fyodor Dostoyevsky (1820-1881), Russia.

Page 160: "Today's problem is not atomic energy but man's heart," Albert Einstein in *I Am with You Always: A Treasury of Inspirational Quotations, Poems, and Prayers,* edited by Douglas Bloch. (New York: Bantam Books, 1998).

Page 162: "In my own lifetime," from *Forgiveness, The Passionate Journey* by Flora Slosson Wuellner. (Nashville: Upper Room Books, 2001). Copyright © 2001 Flora Slosson Wuellner. Used by permission of Upper Room Books.

Page 163: "May the God of justice and mercy unite us," from *Swallow's Nest: A Feminine Reading of the Psalms* by Marchiene Vroon Rienstra. (Grand Rapids, Mich.: Wm. B. Eerdmans Publishing Company, 1992). Copyright © 1992 Wm. B. Eerdmans Publishing Company, Grand Rapids, Mich. Used by permission.

Page 166: "We struggled against one another," South African National Service of Thanksgiving in *An African Prayer Book.* (New York: Doubleday, 1995).

Page 167: "O God, we thank You for this worship time," prayer by Eagle Man, Lakota, from *Worship Resources* by Juanita J. Helphrey. (Excelsior, Minn.: Council for American Indian Ministries, 1991), p. 11.

Page 167: "I am weary of the dark voices," from *Go Tell It on the Mountain* by Robin Green. (England: USPG, 1996). Used by permission of USPG.

Page 168: Luke 19:42 (NRSV)

Page 168: "Come let us go up to the mountain," a Jewish Prayer for Peace from *The Gift of Prayer: A Treasury of Personal Prayer from the World's Spiritual Traditions,* compiled and edited by Jared T. Kieling. (Princeton, New Jersey: Fellowship in Prayer, 1995).

Page 168: "Blessed are the peacemakers," a Christian Prayer for Peace from *The Gift of Prayer: A Treasury of Personal Prayer from the World's Spiritual Traditions,* compiled and edited by Jared T. Kieling. (Princeton, New Jersey: Fellowship in Prayer, 1995).

Page 169: "In a time such as this," from *In the Presence of Fear* by Wendell Berry. (Great Barrington, Ma.: The Orion Society, 2001). Reprinted by permission from *Orion* magazine.

Page 169: "Pray before all else," from "One Prayer for Peace" by Tom Cornell. *Catholic Worker,* Vol. XLVIII, No. 6, Oct.-Nov. 2001. Used by permission of Tom Cornell.

Page 169: "To confront evil successfully," David Spangler in *Peace Prayers: Meditations, Affirmations, Invocations, Poems, and Prayers for Peace,* edited by the staff of HarperSanFrancisco. (New York: HarperCollins Publishers, 1992).

Page 170: "I ask my Lord in the manger," Munib A. Younan, Lutheran Bishop in Jerusalem. www.elca.org.

Page 170: "A special prayer was added by the Serbian Church," Jim Forest in "Icons of Mercy: An Interview with Jim Forest" by Rebecca Laird. *Sacred Journey: The Journal of Fellowship in Prayer;* February 2001, p. 14. Used by permission of Rebecca Laird.

Page 171: "O God of earth and altar," G.K. Chesterton (1874–1936), England.

Page 172: "Where there is gunfire, let there be silence," ("Little Prayer") by Leonardo Alishan in *Christian Science Monitor,* Wednesday, October 31, 2001. Copyright © Leonardo Alishan. Used by permission of Leonardo Alishan.

Page 172: "O God, to those who have hunger give bread," Latin American prayer in *The Gift of Prayer: A Treasury of Personal Prayer from the World's Spiritual Traditions,* compiled and edited by Jared T. Kieling. (Princeton, N.J.: Fellowship in Prayer, 1995).

Page 172: "Throughout the Bible God appears," the Kairos Document, South Africa, in *The Way of Peace,* compiled by Hannah Ward and Jennifer Wild. (Oxford, England: Lion, 1999).

Page 173: "We join with the earth," from *Prayers for Healing* by Pat Mathes Cane. (Berkeley: Conari Press, 1997). Copyright © Patricia Mathes Cane—Capacitar U.N. Environmental Sabbath Program. Used by permission of the author.

Page 174: "Life darkens," from "An American Peace Prayer" by Gregor Stark, Menominee, Wisconsin. Used by permission.

Page 176: "We as 'Peace People' believe in taking down the barriers," Betty Williams from the Nobel Peace Prize acceptance speech, 1976, in *Lutheran Peace Fellowship Supplement to the Manual from Violence to Wholeness*. (Published by Lutheran Peace Fellowship).

Page 176: "Walk together, talk together," Vedic teaching in *The Gift of Prayer: A Treasury of Personal Prayer from the World's Spiritual Traditions*, compiled and edited by Jared T. Kieling. (Princeton, New Jersey: Fellowship in Prayer, 1995).

Page 177: "In a world of flawed communication," from *Caring Enough to Forgive* by David Augsburger. Copyright © 1981 Gospel Light/Regal Books, Ventura, CA 93003. Used by permission.

Page 177: "John of the Cross," from *Good Friday People* by Sheila Cassidy. (Maryknoll, N.Y.: Orbis Books, 1991). Used by permission of Darton, Longman & Todd Ltd. and St. Pauls Philippines. ✒

Page 178: "Having no gift of strategy or arms," Jessica Powers in *The Selected Poetry of Jessica Powers*. (Washington, D.C.: ICS Publications, 1999). All copyrights, Carmelite Monastery, Pewaukee, Wisc. Used by permission.

Page 179: "Pray not for Arab or Jew," Elias Chacour in *Seventy Times Seven: The Power of Forgiveness* by Johann Chistoph Arnold. (Farmington, Penn.: Plough Publishing House, 1997).

Page 179: "Since our inner world is reflected," from "Creating God in the World" by Theresa Magness in *Sacred Journey*, Vol. 51, No. 6, December 2000. Used by permission of Theresa Magness, P.O. Box 460, Junction City, OR 97448. Terrymagness@earthlink.net.

Page 179: "O God, help us not to despise," William Penn.

Page 180: "Breath prayer is my best weapon," Pamela Grenfell Smith in *Women's Uncommon Prayers*, edited by Elizabeth Rankin Geitz, Marjorie A. Burke, and Ann Smith. (Harrisburg, Pa.: Morehouse Publishing, 2000). Copyright © 2000 by Pamela Grenfell Smith. Copying and use by nonprofit groups is permitted and encouraged.

Page 181: "I am the child who lives on the streets," from Children's Aid Direct (slightly adapted) John Carden in *A Procession of Prayers* World Council of Churches, Geneva/Cassell, 1998.

Page 182: "In almost every social studies class," Jim Jarvis in *For the Healing of the Nations: Jubilee Prayer with Global Partners*. Used by permission of Church World Service, P.O. Box 968, Elkhart, IN 46515. 1-800-297-1516. www.churchworldservice.org.

Page 182: "May God bless you with the discomfort at easy answers," Franciscan prayer.

Page 183: "We are amputees," Hem Phang, Kleang Vann, Channa Roth, Chreuk in *For the Healing of the Nations: Jubilee Prayer with Global Partners*, translated by Mr. Seak Meng. Used by permission of Church World Service, P.O. Box 968, Elkhart, IN 46515. 1-800-297-1516. www.churchworldservice.org.

Page 183: "Although the world is full of suffering," Helen Keller in *I Am with You Always: A Treasury of Inspirational Quotations, Poems, and Prayers,* edited by Douglas Bloch. (New York: Bantam Books, 1998).

Page 184: "I give thanks to God," a child's prayer, Puerto Rico, in *Between Heaven and Earth: Prayers and Reflections that Celebrate an Intimate God,* compiled and edited by Ken Gire. (New York: HarperCollins Publishers, 1997).

Page 184: "May the God who cares passionately for the earth," from *Swallow's Nest: A Feminine Reading of the Psalms* by Marchiene Vroon Rienstra. (Grand Rapids, Mich.: Wm. B. Eerdmans Publishing Company, 1992). Copyright © 1992 Wm. B. Eerdmans Publishing Company, Grand Rapids, Michigan. Used by permission.

Page 185: "The year was the decade-maker, 1970," Richard Wilcox in *Gifts of Many Cultures: Worship Resources for the Global Community,* edited by Maren C. Tirabassi and Kathy Wonson Eddy. (Cleveland: United Church Press, 1995).

Page 185: "Blessed be," Ancient Celtic blessing.

For Further Reading

Books with a in the acknowledgments section include some of the best personal stories, biblical context, psychological dimensions of difficult issues, and Christian spirituality that I found in reading for this book.

Every effort has been made to trace and acknowledge copyright holders of all the prayers and readings in this anthology. We apologize for any errors or omissions that may remain, and ask those concerned to contact the publishers, who will make full acknowledgment in the future.

OTHER RESOURCES FROM AUGSBURG BOOKS

Soul Weavings: A Gathering of Women's Prayers
by Lyn Klug
160 pages, 0-8066-2849-9

A collection of rich, strong prayers that reflect the needs and experiences of women of all ages. They are gathered from historic and comtemporary women of faith from around the world.

All Will Be Well: A Gathering of Healing Prayers
by Lyn Klug
176 pages, 0-8066-3729-3

A gathering of prayers that will help many speak the words of their hearts as they pray for healing in their own and others' lives.

Psalms for Healing
by Gretchen Person
176 pages, 0-8066-4161-4

A thoughtful collection of the most helpful passages from the psalms for those seeking healing. Organized by specific emotions, situations, and events, this is a resource that patients, family, and caregivers will treasure and use.

Available wherever books are sold.